Collingwood's The Idea of History

BLOOMSBURY READER'S GUIDES

Bloomsbury Reader's Guides are clear, concise and accessible introductions to key texts. Each book explores the themes, context, criticism and influence of key works, providing a practical introduction to close reading, guiding students towards a thorough understanding of the text. They provide an essential, up-to-date resource, ideal for undergraduate students.

READER'S GUIDES

Collingwood's The Idea of History

A Reader's Guide

PETER JOHNSON

B L O O M S B U R Y

LONDON • NEW DELHI • NEW YORK • SYDNEY

Bloomsbury Academic

An imprint of Bloomsbury Publishing Plc

50 Bedford Square
London
WC1B 3DP
UK

175 Fifth Avenue
New York
NY 10010
USA

www.bloomsbury.com

First published 2013

British Library Cataloguing-in-Publication Data
A catalogue record for this book is available from the British Library.

ISBN: HB: 978-1-4411-4177-4
PB: 978-1-4411-5123-0

Typeset by Fakenham Prepress Solutions, Fakenham, Norfolk NR21 8NN
Printed and bound in India

CONTENTS

ACKNOWLEDGEMENTS

This Reader's Guide is aimed at aiding students who come to R. G. Collingwood's *The Idea of History* for the first time. Even so, in writing it I have been helped more than once by those writers on Collingwood for whom understanding his thought has been a lifetime's project. I am deeply indebted to all the commentators on Collingwood's writings, especially those who have not held back on criticism of his ideas. In terms of exegesis two labourers in the Collingwood vineyard stand out – William H. Dray and Jan van der Dussen – since their efforts in making Collingwood's philosophy of history accessible in a comprehensive form is what has made modern interpretations of it possible. Naturally, any errors of understanding are my own.

TEXT

The edition used throughout (IH) is R. G. Collingwood, *The Idea of History*, Revised Edition, With Lectures 1926–1928, edited with an Introduction by Jan van der Dussen, Clarendon Press, Oxford, 1993 (paperback, Oxford University Press, 1994)

'Were they like that?' Isa asked abruptly. 'The Victorians,' Mrs Swithin mused. 'I don't believe', she said with her odd little smile, 'that there ever were such people. Only you and me and William dressed differently.' 'You don't believe in history', said William.

VIRGINIA WOOLF. (1941) BETWEEN THE ACTS

ABBREVIATIONS

A	An Autobiography
IH	The Idea of History
PA	The Principles of Art
PE	The Philosophy of Enchantment
PH	The Principles of History
SM	Speculum Mentis

INTRODUCTION

R. G. Collingwood's *The Idea of History* is a remarkable book. It has an author's name and a title, but the title is one the author chose for a different purpose and he had no say in arranging the book's contents. For *The Idea of History* was published in 1946, some three years after its author's death, but, unlike *The Idea of Nature* which also appeared posthumously, Collingwood's major work on the philosophy of history is not a continuous piece of writing, but a collection of material put together by somebody else.

These facts about *The Idea of History* are well known and have not affected its status as one of the enduring works of twentieth-century philosophy. Students of the philosophy of history turn to Collingwood with as much expectation as students of aesthetics search out his other ground-breaking text, *The Principles of Art*. Collingwood's work is made seminal by its arguments and the understanding of history these arguments support. His reflections on history are radical and he wished to present them in a manner which reflected their philosophical distinctiveness, but in the face of multiplying obstacles his road ahead became increasingly uncertain, so there is a sense in which Collingwood's writings on the philosophy of history lack a completely finished pattern. They are open to reconstruction, but they are also prone to misunderstanding. By sorting out the arguments about history that Collingwood means to defend from those with which he has been wrongly burdened, the Reader's Guide aims to help students of Collingwood to understand and criticize his ideas. Equally, by explaining the development of Collingwood's thinking about history the Guide aims to show how and when he arrived at his views, together with the understandings of history he rejects.

There is no doubt about the importance that Collingwood attaches to history. Of all the problems faced by modern philosophy he believed that the problem of history – its nature, aims and methods – was the most pressing. It is true, of course, that Collingwood wrote on art, religion and philosophy itself with a close to equivalent urgency, but he believed that history had been made the poor relation of modern philosophy and it was because he believed this that he undertook the philosophical re-examination of history as his life's work. Rather more startlingly, perhaps, Collingwood also believed that the nature of history was too singular a topic to be left to the authority of professional historians. Collingwood was a renowned archaeologist and historian of Roman Britain, but while his philosophy of history is heavily concerned with the methodology of historical enquiry he argues almost to the point of perversity that history's importance does not derive exclusively from what historians do. The actual practice of historical writing is certainly vital, but in Collingwood's hands history is not the personal possession of historians. Human beings are temporal creatures. They live at a particular historical time, and their lives are framed in terms of memory and imagination as well as expectation and hope. In this sense, for Collingwood, history is less like a specialized form of knowledge than a basis for common understanding. The activities of my neighbour in her front garden on a Sunday morning in June, deciphering a Roman inscription, reading a nineteenth-century diary, tracking the movements of French troops across the terrain north of Paris during the battle of the Marne, are each exercises in historical understanding. Collingwood's response to the neglect of history has the effect of raising our aspirations for it.

Collingwood's philosophical investment in history is made largely to counter the belief that natural science is the paradigm form of knowledge. Take this belief as a working assumption for understanding the lives of human beings both past and present and much of human life becomes unintelligible. Historical understanding is an essential part of human understanding, and human understanding is what separates human beings from nature. The eruptions of volcanoes, the frequency of tidal waves both admit of chronologies, but chronologies are not history. Similarly, natural events can be explained causally, sometimes with the aim of constructing laws which allow predictions to be made, but human intentions are not like natural events and so they cannot be explained like them either. Given that Collingwood's philosophy of history is based on a sharp distinction between history and science, we may be surprised by his insistence that it is as a science that he wishes history to be recovered. But history does not become a science by aping natural science. Rather it becomes a science only through a greater self-consciousness of its autonomy. It is the distinctiveness of history that is the source of its creativity and its capacity for systematic understanding.

Philosophers often boast that they never discover anything. Certainly, Collingwood's discovery of the autonomy of history is not like splitting the atom or locating a new species of butterfly in the rain forests of Brazil. Even so, what Collingwood's philosophy of history discloses is nothing less than the logical basis of history and the vocabulary appropriate to it. He tells us how human beings think of their past, and he identifies the concepts that are necessary if his account is to be convincing. Thus, Collingwood speaks about historical re-enactment and about the sense in which the past is embedded in the present in the form of evidence. He speaks, too, about the role of the imagination in historical enquiry and about the logic of question and answer which is in his eyes the replacement for propositional logic and also the best account we have of how historical investigations actually work.

What a philosophy of history should aim at is established early. The job of philosophy is to reveal the logical character of the experience it is investigating. Since human understanding is diverse both in nature and object, what philosophy investigates may be the physical world and the scientific laws which govern it, the human world and the moral beliefs that are found in it, our religious beliefs or our ability to find some things beautiful and others not. Human activities presuppose criteria of understanding. The aim of philosophy is to tell us what these are. It is to reveal principles that are already implicit in experience. Philosophy proceeds in ways that are distinctive and it is self-reflective where art, science and history are not. It is, therefore, uniquely placed to distinguish the ways by which we understand the world.

The idea at work in *The Idea of History* is, then, a philosopher's idea and as a preparation for the efforts ahead Collingwood tells us that history is to be distinguished in terms of its nature, object, method and value. History is first a form of enquiry. Its aim is to find things out by putting the material under investigation to the test. Second, history's object is the past and this tells us what kinds of things historians mean to discover. They are, as Collingwood puts it, 'the actions of human beings as they have been done in the past' (IH 9). Third, history's methods are the collection and interpretation of evidence. Since the past is over, to be known at all it must be known indirectly, and this means through the availability of evidence. Finally, Collingwood answers his own question – What is history for? It is a form of self-knowledge. What human beings are capable of can be established only by looking at what they have done. Erase history and you take away human identity.

The job of a philosophy of history, then, is to show how history is possible given its distinctive object, method and value. No philosophy of history can proceed without a thorough knowledge of how historians and archaeologists go about their work. Collingwood himself was uniquely placed here, being a philosopher and an historian as well as a hugely experienced archaeologist. But the questions which are asked by historians and archaeologists are not the questions which philosophers ask. As Collingwood explains it himself, 'for the philosopher, the fact demanding attention is neither the past by itself, as it is for the historian, nor the historian's thought about it by itself, as it is for the psychologist, but the two things in their mutual relation' (IH 2). The point is beautifully made. In teasing out the concepts which make art, science and history what they are, philosophers need to understand how artists, scientists and historians actually work, but they do not become artists, scientists and historians in doing so.

In the light of Collingwood's determination to express historical knowledge as both autonomous and systematic it may seem odd that his thought about history has often been associated with relativism – the belief that truth is relative to given conceptual schemes and conceptual schemes can be traced historically, but not evaluated or compared since there is no standpoint from which we can make such an evaluation, apart from another conceptual scheme. The charge of relativism is one which we shall examine, but what should be clear is just how remote it is from the general character of Collingwood's intentions. For Collingwood saw no point in weighing history down with a certainty which it could not deliver. False objectivity does not protect history from scepticism, and in history objectivity is false if it asks that the past is reproduced rather than re-enacted. Collingwood's philosophy of history aims to show how systematic historical knowledge is possible, but it insists also that it is not possible at all if we think of it in terms of scientific laws or law-like generalizations.

The rules which govern the acquisition of historical knowledge are demanding and intricate, but any attempt to show what these are will fail if it takes scientific objectivity – the testing of hypotheses by replication and the re-examination of data – as the only model for truth. Indeed, Collingwood goes out of his way to point out that this picture of historical knowledge as the establishment of fact is substantially incomplete. History is not just about lists of dates – the Kings and Queens of England, say, or the Reform Acts; nor is it just about events and the causes of events – the Battle of Britain in the summer of 1940, say, or the assassination of an American President. Nor is history about the treatment of past experience as fact, since facts do not come to historians with their explanations already made. In Collingwood's view, facts figure on the historian's radar only after a complex process of inference has taken place. Similarly, events – say, Napoleon's retreat from Moscow or the introduction of conscription in Britain in 1916 – will remain closed to historical understanding unless the historian can reconstruct the thoughts they involve. For, unlike the natural scientist, what confronts the historian is not a subject that can be investigated by means of experiment under controlled conditions, but a past, a region of experience which no longer exists, one which we cannot sensibly think of as repeatable in any significant way. Moreover, it is a past which it is the business of history to understand when recall and memory are superfluous to the task at hand.

R. G. Collingwood was a working historian and archaeologist for almost the whole of his life. Not afraid to get his hands dirty or to direct excavations himself, Collingwood, under the early guidance of his father W. G. Collingwood, and with the encouragement of his mentor at Oxford Francis Haverfield, became one of the leading historians of Roman Britain. He had long and often hard experience of excavation and he worked with many of the founding fathers of Romano-British archaeology. Collingwood always saw theory in close conjunction with practice. Whether it was an exercise in the history of ideas, such as the history of the idea of history which makes up Part I of *The Idea of History*, or a survey of the economic practices of Ancient Rome, Collingwood's operating principle was that neither can be grasped without an appreciation of the idea or the practice involved. We know, too (A 30), that Collingwood's account of history was shaped by insights gained from his own experience of tackling historical problems. As an historian in such works as *Roman Britain* (1923, with a second and largely rewritten edition following in 1932) and *Roman Britain and the English Settlements* (1936, in which he wrote the first four books), Collingwood told the story of the Roman invasion and occupation of Britain from the point of view of the occupiers and the occupied. As an archaeologist in such works as *The Archaeology of Roman Britain* (1930) and in many articles published in the *Transactions of the Cumberland and Westmorland Antiquarian and Archaeological Society* and elsewhere, Collingwood published the results of his work on Hadrian's Wall and a host of other archaeological subjects. Much of Collingwood's historical work is devoted to explaining the material conditions of life in Roman Britain and the Roman Empire. Social and economic conditions, industries such as mining, population movements and statistics and land use, together with military history, are all fruitful subjects of Collingwood's historical investigation.

The influence of Collingwood's idea of history on his own way of writing history and on his own archaeological practice (and, indeed, on the writing and practices of others) is an important topic of discussion. Even so, the nature of Collingwood's principles of history stands independently. Their origin, substance and validity are matters for philosophy. They deal with problems which it is outside the remit of either history or archaeology to solve. Throughout his life Collingwood worked on philosophy, history and archaeology. He was keen to investigate the links between them, but no one was interchangeable with the others. While archaeology gives history its empirical methodology it is not history itself, and while history gives philosophy the past as the subject matter of the philosophy of history it cannot on its own say what the past is, nor what makes history a valid form of experience in understanding it.

As a philosopher, then, Collingwood's interest in history is with the conditions which make historical knowledge possible, but he also believed that history matters because a society that loses its sense of the past has also lost an essential element of its own identity. A human past is not wholly remote from the present, but

is experience which the present may wish to live down, live up
to, deny or emulate. None of these responses would be possible
if the past could not be reconstructed or could be thought of
only on the model of natural science. Thus it is not surprising
that Collingwood thinks of history as bearing the closest possible
relation to life. Equally, history could not bear a close relation to
life if historical knowledge was thought of solely as a body of fact
or as data or information. To learn from history has sense only if
the past is construed in terms of thought – whether it is the thought
in the mind of the recruiting sergeant standing on the high street of
an English town in late August 1914 or a Greek general contemplating the invasion of Sicily in the fifth century BC.

A NOTE ABOUT READING

The main texts on Collingwood which discuss his philosophy of history, including works specifically on his philosophy of history, are listed below. These will appear in the reading lists (under Further reading at the end of the book) as the author followed by page number, together with the main articles that have been written on each topic.

Main texts

D'Oro, Giuseppina. (2002), *Collingwood and the Metaphysics of Experience*, London: Routledge.

Dray, William H. (1995), *History as Re-enactment: R. G. Collingwood's Idea of History*, Oxford: Clarendon Press.

Helgeby, Stein. (2004), *Action as History, The Historical Thought of R. G. Collingwood*, Exeter: Imprint Academic.

Hinz, Michael. (1994), *Self-Creation and History, Collingwood and Nietzsche on Conceptual Change*, Lanham, MD: University Press of America.

Hughes-Warrington, Marnie. (2003), '*How Good an Historian Shall I Be?*' *R. G. Collingwood, The Historical Imagination and Education*, Exeter: Imprint Academic.

Johnson, Peter. (1998), *R. G. Collingwood*, Bristol: Thoemmes Press.

Kanichai, Cyriac. (1981), *R. G. Collingwood's Philosophy of History*, Alwaye: Pontifical Institute of Theology and Philosophy.

Leach, Stephen. (2009), *The Foundations of History, Collingwood's Analysis of Historical Explanation*, Exeter: Imprint Academic.

Martin, Rex. (1977), *Historical Explanation, Re-Enactment and Practical Inference*, Ithaca, NY: Cornell University Press.

Mink, Louis. O. (1969), *Mind, History and Dialectic, The Philosophy of R. G. Collingwood*, Bloomington: University of Indiana Press.

Rubinoff, L. (1970), *Collingwood and the Reform of Metaphysics, A Study in the Philosophy of Mind*, Toronto: University of Toronto Press.

Russell, Anthony F. (1984), *Logic, Philosophy, and History, A Study in the Philosophy of History Based on the Work of R. G. Collingwood*, Lanham, MD: University Press of America.

Saari, Heikki. (1984), *Re-enactment: A Study in R. G. Collingwood's Philosophy of History*, Abo: Abo Akademi.

Skagestad, Peter. (1975), *Making Sense of History – the Philosophies of Popper and Collingwood*, Oslo: Universitetsforlaget.

Van der Dussen, W. J. (1981), *History as a Science: The Philosophy of R.G. Collingwood*, The Hague: Martinus Nijhoff.

Books that include substantial discussions of Collingwood's philosophy of history

Browning, Gary K. (2004), *Rethinking R. G. Collingwood, Philosophy, Politics and the Unity of Theory and Practice*, Basingstoke: Palgrave Macmillan.

Dray, William. (1957), *Laws and Explanation in History*, Oxford: Oxford University Press.

—(1980), *Perspectives on History*, London: Routledge & Kegan Paul.

—(1989), *On History and Philosophers of History*, Leiden: E. J. Brill.

Gallie, W. B. (1964), *Philosophy and the Historical Understanding*, London: Chatto & Windus.

Gardiner, Patrick. (1952), *The Nature of Historical Explanation*, Oxford: Oxford University Press.

Goldstein, Leon J. (1976), *Historical Knowing*, Austin: University of Texas Press.

Mandelbaum, Maurice. (1977), *The Anatomy of Historical Knowledge*, Baltimore, MD: Johns Hopkins University Press.

Mink, Louis O. (1987), *Historical Understanding*, London: Cornell University Press.

Parker, Christopher. (2000), *The English Idea of History from Coleridge to Collingwood*, Aldershot: Ashgate.

Pompa, L. and Dray, W. H. (eds). (1981), *Substance and Form in History*, Edinburgh: University of Edinburgh Press.

Van der Dussen, W. J. and Rubinoff, Lionel (eds). (1991), *Objectivity, Method and Point of View, Essays in the Philosophy of History*, Leiden: E. J. Brill.

CHAPTER ONE

Background to the text

Text

Collingwood's *The Idea of History* is not an uncomplicated text. It is not wholly the book which Collingwood intended to write on history and it consists of material written at different times and for different purposes. Thus to make it less complicated we need to establish what Collingwood's intentions were and then get a clearer picture of the book's content.

In 2012 we are in a much better position to understand Collingwood's plans for the publication of his writings on history than would have been possible in 1946, and, indeed, for a number of years afterwards. What Collingwood actually intended is unambiguously laid out in letters he wrote to the Clarendon Press, Oxford in June and October 1939 (see Peter Johnson, *The Correspondence of R. G. Collingwood, An Illustrated Guide*, The R. G. Collingwood Society, 1998, Letters C2lxxv and C2lxxix). What Collingwood planned was a series of volumes divided into three categories: (1) *Philosophical Essays* to consist of *An Essay on Philosophical Method* (published in 1933) and *An Essay on Metaphysics*, (published in 1940); (2) *Philosophical Principles* to consist of *The Principles of Art* (published in 1938) and *The Principles of History* (parts of which were published in *The Idea of History* in 1946 and much of the remainder, together with other material in 1999), and (3) *Studies in the History of Ideas* to consist of *The Idea of Nature* (published in 1945) and *The Idea of History* (published in 1946).

From this plan we can see that, as originally intended, *The Idea of History* was to cover the history of ideas about history from the ancient world to the modern, roughly the material concerning historiography on which Collingwood had lectured in Oxford in 1936 (and other years) and which is included in Parts I to IV of the book as it was later published in its edited form. We can be sure that Collingwood's design of his series was not accidental. For whereas his aim in the History of Ideas category is to give an account of the historical emergence of the idea of history (or of the idea of nature), together with their evolution and development, the goal of Philosophical Principles is quite different. Here his objective is to show what it is that makes art or history possible at all. Just as Collingwood's aesthetics in *The Principles of Art* aims to establish the nature of art proper as opposed to a number of false approximations of it, so his *Principles of History* aims to reveal the autonomy of historical understanding by distinguishing it from ways of thinking that are unable to capture history's true character. In other words, both works are intended to make us think about the inner rationale of the activities they examine.

Collingwood believed that to get to grips with history, both approaches were necessary. Mapping the conceptual boundaries of history is not an activity that could be conducted out of the blue. Equally, Collingwood interjects his history of the ideas of history with comments aimed at revealing the adequacy of any given idea. We may readily assume that this is why Collingwood planned the history and the principles to appear together in two separate volumes. What we should not assume, however, is that this gives us anything more than a hint about the philosophical issues at stake. Publishing the two volumes in tandem does give us a strong indication of the close relation philosophy bears with history, but it is only an arrangement of thought, not the thought itself.

Why, then, were Collingwood's writings on history made public in the form of *The Idea of History*, a text which is something of a problem text, rather than as he would have wished? The words contained in *The Idea of History* are Collingwood's own and the text is not deliberately ambiguous, but it is a composite work, some parts of which are finished, others very much less so, including sections of *The Principles of History* itself. It is not that Collingwood did not try to complete *The Principles of History*. In 1939 during a recuperative voyage to the Dutch East Indies he wrote a little over one-third of it. But then work stopped. In fact, the answer is suggested in the date of Collingwood's voyage and the reason for it. In 1939 Collingwood was suffering from a progressively debilitating illness. He knew that if he was to finish the work he had planned he would have to work fast, and he also knew that some projects would have to be sacrificed. By 1939 Collingwood was aware that the coming Second World War was inevitable. He needed to speak out, and so he formed the intention to write another work about principles, this time the fundamental principles of a liberal politics. This was *The New Leviathan* (published in 1942). It occupied Collingwood up until the last year of his life and we have good reason for thinking that this is the book which *The Principles of History* was set aside to complete.

After Collingwood died early in 1943 it was felt that the writings on nature and history made the best case for publication. Whereas the nature manuscript was self-contained the material on history was diverse, and the job of editing it and preparing it for publication was given to a student and friend of Collingwood's, T. M. Knox. It was Knox, then, who had the task of bringing *The Idea of History*, as it was to be called, into the world. This he did in 1946. Knox selected manuscript material for publication by reference: first, to how finished he thought it was, and second, to the availability of the content elsewhere in Collingwood's published writing, especially in his *An Autobiography* which had been published in 1939.

Knox's Preface to the 1946 edition, together with Jan van der Dussen's invaluable Editor's Introduction to his 1993 revised edition of *The Idea of History*, tell us a great deal about how the volume, was composed. Knox's first decision was to publish Collingwood's writings on history in one volume rather than two as had been originally planned. His second was to divide the volume into two sections, one on historiography (Parts I to IV), and the other on the philosophical principles of history (Part V). While Collingwood had revised a small part of the first section in 1940, it was more or less complete, being the main body of the lectures on the subject he gave in 1936. Part V was a very different matter, however. To some degree following Collingwood's own title, Knox called Part V, Epilegomena. Here Knox decided to include material from Collingwood's 1936 Lectures concerning the nature of historical knowledge, together with material from Chapters 1 and 4 of the unfinished manuscript of *The Principles of History*. To this Knox added two published items, *The Historical Imagination*, Collingwood's Inaugural Lecture which had been published in 1935, and *Human Nature and Human History*, a lecture to the British Academy which had been published in 1936.

Summing this up, the Epilegomena section consists of work produced between 1935 and 1939, some of which was published, some not. Some of this takes the form of essays and lectures, some manuscript material from the unfinished *The Principles of History*. The division of Part V into seven subsections was also Knox's, as was the ordering of the material it contained. Thus, we have the Epilegomena as Knox entitled and presented it.

1 *Human Nature and Human History* 1936
2 *The Historical Imagination* 1935
3 'Historical Evidence', Chapter 1 of the unfinished *The Principles of History* 1939
4 'History as the Re-enactment of Past Experience' 1936 Lectures
5 'The Subject-matter of History' 1936 Lectures
6 'History and Freedom', part of Chapter 4 of *The Principles of History* 1939
7 'Progress as Created by Historical Thinking' 1936 Lectures

Research on Collingwood's manuscripts has revealed grounds for disagreement with Knox's procedures, but I think that two points need to be made here. First, there is a strong sense in which Collingwood's philosophical insights about the nature of history rise above their edited format. The doctrines central to Collingwood's account of history emerge clearly from *The Idea of History*, and while they often provoke a considerable degree of argument, including, sometimes, opposition, their meaning is, more often than not, quite transparent. This is not to say that some topics, re-enactment, for example, are always treated exhaustively, nor is it to deny that fringe topics, such as the relation between history and biography, are given more attention outside *The Idea of History* than in it. Second, there is an equally strong sense in which debates about the adequacy of Knox's edition are of limited interest because since the publication in 1999 of *The Principles of History* together with the incorporation of much relevant additional material, there is little of Collingwood's writing on history that is now outside the public domain. Collingwood's writings on history, if not in the form he intended, are now completely open to discussion and debate.

Context

While Herodotus is considered to be the father of history, we can reasonably think of Collingwood as the originator of modern philosophical accounts of history. Yet, Collingwood was resistant to modern analytical philosophy, and so his account of the emergence of history as an autonomous form of understanding is largely conducted independently. What interests Collingwood is not history consisting of statements which can be tested against scientific criteria, but the idea of history itself. Even so, the thought that historians are in some sense concerned with ascertainable fact is not easily set aside. So when Collingwood turns to the history of ideas of history he is careful to acknowledge what is true as well as what is false in theories of history which take verifiability as their model.

To express this point more generally. The best method for setting *The Idea of History* in context is to turn to the history of ideas of history in the first four parts of the book. This discussion of Graeco-Roman historiography, the rise of Christian ideas of history, of the approach of scientific history and of scientific history itself is important to philosophers as well as to historians of ideas, since in these sections Collingwood does more than just identify the salient characteristics of the thinking about history in each period. He plots the development of the idea of history as an autonomous discipline of thought, and so he charts lines of progress and regression, startlingly new insights which find themselves repeated in later ways of thinking, as well as relapses and setbacks in which history finds itself embraced by understandings which are not its own. In other words, there is a significant sense in which Collingwood wants his readers to understand his survey as leading to the completion of his own point of view. Given that Collingwood's history of the ideas of history was originally given as lectures, this is not, perhaps, surprising. Not only does Collingwood's thinking about historiography parallel and also inform his investigations into the nature of history, we do not go far wrong in concluding that he intended that it should.

Once Collingwood's general approach has been grasped, we can see how it works in individual cases. Thus, in Collingwood's hands (IH 17–20), the historical writings of Herodotus do not simply chronicle his own age. They contain in embryonic form some of the elements of autonomy that the modern understanding of history requires. An ancient historian's view of evidence as the testimony of eyewitnesses for the occurrence of a particular event – say, the death of an individual in battle – is an advance because it allows the eyewitness account to be tested, thus permitting the historian to move from the belief that the death occurred to the knowledge that it has. But, equally, this ancient understanding of evidence is limited to what testimony can provide and this in turn limits the scope of history. Collingwood thought that the interrogation of eyewitness accounts was a development of the first importance in the emergence of the idea of history. Limited in range, it provided nevertheless an essential feature of scientific history as Collingwood understands it, namely a critical method for the establishment of fact.

We see a similar technique in Collingwood's treatment of the English Renaissance historian and philosopher Francis Bacon (IH 58–60). What Bacon achieved was the identification of the past as past, as an area of human experience worth studying for its own sake rather than as the manifestation of a divine plan or as the function of the divine will. But Bacon limited history by restricting it to what could be recovered by memory. Thus, in addition to the project of understanding the past as past, what was needed was a critical method for carrying this out. To restrict history to the remembered past is to look at the past with one eye closed. Thus, while it is the past as past which the historian is interested in reconstructing, systematic rules and procedures are needed to achieve this when memory is absent.

In Collingwood's account the emergence of history as an autonomous discipline of thought is neither smooth nor settled.

There are periods when the idea is grasped only dimly or where it is outweighed by lack of the necessary practical or technical skills. But there are also times when the ingenuity of a particular individual presses the idea forward, massively anticipating understandings of history which only come to be appreciated later. Collingwood thought that Vico was such an individual. In fact, on T. M. Knox's account, Collingwood used to say that if Plato was his favourite philosopher it was Vico who had influenced him the most (IH viii). His philosophy was the subject of Collingwood's first book, a translation of a work by the modern Italian philosopher Benedetto Croce, *The Philosophy of Giambattista Vico*, published by Howard Latimer in London in 1913, an event that conveniently links Vico to Croce as two of the most important influences on Collingwood's views.

Working in eighteenth-century Naples, Vico developed a way of thinking about history which was as revolutionary in his time as Collingwood's was in his. Through Vico's inspiration the idea of history overcame Cartesian scepticism and so cleared the way for history as a distinct human science which offered both knowledge and practical wisdom. Collingwood writes about Vico with verve and affection. In the first place, Vico was an historian who knew the problems of historical research from the inside. Collingwood thought that it was impossible to get to grips with any activity, theoretical or practical, unless one had long and hard experience of it. Theories of boat building, for instance, were useless without the actual experience of shaping the hull or situating the masts. The same is true of history. Vico passes this test with scarcely a murmur of doubt on Collingwood's part.

On Vico's substantive contribution Collingwood is firm, but he adds reservations. What Vico saw clearly was that history has no existence at all if it is thought of as the apprehension of fact. First, in human understanding, facts do not come alive until the ideas internal to them are grasped. Second, the appropriate question to ask of human activities is not whether they are true or false, but what they mean. Almost at a stroke Vico sweeps away a host of assumptions about historical method. Historians do not proceed by reference to testimony, but by putting testimony to the test. Records, documents, inscriptions are no longer to be considered as authorities but witnesses to be questioned. The aim is to recon- struct the past on its own terms, but the means for achieving this are no longer the cutting and pasting of sources, but the active interrogating power of the historical mind itself. Vico switches the focus from what is known to how we know it. It is a move of extraordinary power and significance, since its result is to make history critical. Sources are not self-authenticating, but conditional on their capacity to yield answers to the historian's questions. It is, in other words, the historian who reigns.

Through Vico's discoveries the idea of history ceases to be the poor relation of empiricism. Once the narrow conception of the facts is abandoned, historians are able to deploy a wide range of human material from myths to fairy-tales and the practices of primitive societies. However, as Collingwood insists, while this move to make history critical was a major step forward, much more was required. Vico had shown that the imagination of the historian was the key to the very possibility of history itself. He had shown that to expect from history a level of certainty beyond the narratives of the past that historians construct is to expect what history cannot provide. History is the product of the historical mind. This is what makes it critical. We do not yet know what makes criticism scientific, but Vico's revolution was an advance, one which Collingwood was keen to identify as such.

Croce's book on Vico introduces a more immediate context to *The Idea of History*. Collingwood saw the history of the idea of history and the influences on his own thought in very much the same light, and he shares Croce's tendency to understand earlier conceptions of history as stepping stones to his own. We might think of this as a deliberate philosophical technique, one that both philosophers acquired from Hegel. Collingwood and Croce wrote against the broad philosophical background of Hegel's own works, and the tradition of nineteenth-century Hegelianism which they inherited. Not that either Collingwood or Croce ever read Hegel except through their own intellectual needs and circumstances. Thus, the Hegelian understanding of human experience in terms of a comprehensive phenomenology which reveals the unity behind diverse modes of thinking and acting is one which to various degrees in specific periods of his writing Collingwood followed. On its own, however, this project does not pin down exactly what makes history different. It certainly tells us that a mode of understanding which works very well in ordering one type of experience will fail completely when faced with another. Hegel's opposition to naturalism, therefore, is to be counted an advance because it captures the sense in which the historian is concerned with actions rather than with events or happenings. But the actions which are the subject matter of history are past actions and so the historian's problem is how to breathe life into a past which is now dead. By a similar token, Collingwood's problem, as a philosopher as well as an historian, is how to make sense of history as an activity which delivers knowledge of the past, as opposed to beliefs, guesses or intuitions about it.

Collingwood believed that with Hegel (together with a number of other late eighteenth- and nineteenth-century thinkers examined in Part III of *The Idea of History*), we reach the threshold of scientific history. Why? To answer this question we must retrace our steps a little. Scientific history (or history proper as we might understand it, using Collingwood's language in *The Principles of Art*), arises out of dissatisfaction with the commonsense solution to the problem of historical knowledge. On the commonsense view the acquisition of historical knowledge looks like this. The historian wishes to arrive at an account of the past – say, the storming of the Bastille during the French Revolution – which is factually correct. Since it is obviously impossible for historians to be observers of this experience they must rely on the observations of those who were there at the time. Thus, the testimony of participants becomes the essential raw material of history. On this basis, the commonsense view concludes that the job of the historian is to collect testimony, to select and rearrange it, and sometimes to reject it as inconsistent or unsound. Collingwood argues, however, that the collection of testimony is not history but chronicle. Chronicle is history falsely understood. Even so, chronicle contains the hint of history proper because the historian, in choosing between testimonies, is not a passive recipient of them but actually bringing them to life. With the arrival of critical history the hint of history proper becomes stronger. Sources are no longer authorities in their own right, but evidence open to interrogation by the historian. Moreover, the historian is as much concerned with the criteria according to which sources are judged as with the sources themselves. For what is important about historical knowledge is not factual information alone, but the cluster of social meanings which bring the facts to life.

By placing the imagination of the historian, together with the critical procedures necessary for the examination of sources at the centre of history, Collingwood brings critical history to the borders of history proper. To put this point another way. Critical history certainly finesses chronicle, but it is a horse from the same stable nevertheless. And the reason for this is that critical history is still not radical enough because it leaves two crucial questions unanswered. First, how can historians bring the past to life when, as critical history requires, they write about it from the perspective of the present? Second, how can historians arrive at historical knowledge if they treat their subject matter not as data to be established as true or false, but as action? Not without qualification, Collingwood believed Hegel had teased out the beginnings of the answers to both questions.

In 1906 a book by Croce was published (the third Italian edition of 1912 was translated into English in 1915), called *What is Living and What is Dead in the Philosophy of Hegel*. The title is instructive because it tells us a great deal about how Croce and Collingwood saw the history of philosophy. Past thought is not remote from present philosophical concerns, but rather a spur to a conversation which brings the past to life by engaging with it on its own terms and by estimating its place in the development of ideas. Thus, for Collingwood in *The Idea of History*, what is important about Hegel's philosophy of the spirit is its capacity to move our understanding of history forward. What is living in Hegel's understanding of history is his recognition that what concerns the historian is not the past as such, since there is no possibility of the past being regained, but the past as ending in the present. Since the future is also closed to historical enquiry the historian's business is always present business. This does not mean the glorification of the present. As Collingwood pithily remarks, 'History *must* end with the present, because nothing else has happened' (IH 120). If Hegel's thinking here helps with the first question that critical history left unanswered it does also with the second. Hegel argued, in Collingwood's view correctly, that there can be no history except human history. Moreover, events in human history – a naval battle, the discovery of penicillin, an abdication crisis – cannot be understood at all unless the reasons behind them are grasped. Events are open to history only as the outward expression of thought. Two difficulties follow from this. Both raise problems for Hegel and, interestingly, for Collingwood, too. First, if the mainspring of history is reason, what place is there in history for human emotions? Second, if history is fundamentally a rational process, what place is there in history for the absence of reason? Neither Hegel nor Collingwood see much role in history for causal explanations. Human intentions are not to be understood, as Hegel puts it with heavy emphasis, as the phrenologist explains bumps on the head. Both are drawn towards history as the expression of thought which means that they need some account of the capacity of history to encompass experience which is human, but also arbitrary, accidental or illogical. We shall return to these problems later, but it is worth noticing that Collingwood does not consider that these difficulties make Hegel's insights any less valuable. All history remains the history of thought. Equally, all history remains present history. Where Hegel's discussion of history is deadening in Collingwood's view is in its support for a universal history, the picture of the historical process as following a single, speculative idea. What troubles Collingwood about this is that it distracts the historian from the evidence. For Collingwood, the notion of historical evidence is a vitally important element in history understood as a special science. It is Hegel's relative neglect of this which marks his separation from history proper.

We will now turn to the contemporary context of *The Idea of History*. This is important because in it Collingwood converses with his peers. Thus, in Part IV of the work Collingwood discusses developments in historical thinking in England, Germany, France and Italy from the last quarter of the nineteenth century to his own day, as in the earlier sections treating these ideas as forerunners. History, as Collingwood understands it, relates past thought to the historian's own. Thus, the philosophers and historians Collingwood speaks with include major figures in the history of historical understanding such as F. H. Bradley and Michael Oakeshott in England, Dilthey and Spengler in Germany, Bergson in France and Croce in Italy, as well as a number of figures now long forgotten, such as the nineteenth-century historian Robert Mackenzie, author of a book on progress, who even Collingwood deems unappealing (IH 145).

In F.H. Bradley, by contrast, Collingwood meets a philosopher whose reflections on the nature of history (as expressed in his *The Presuppositions of Critical History* 1874) are seminal. Bradley nears the full understanding of history understood as a critical discipline of thought. Collingwood, therefore, places him among those who see history as scientific, in Collingwood's special sense. But what Bradley omits is exactly the frame of reference which Collingwood aims to supply, namely the grasp of history as constructive as well as critical. Thus, history is a science not in the sense of natural science but as the critical and constructive discovery of past thought.

Bradley points towards this modern renaissance in history because he sees that history does not hold a mirror to the past, but embraces it through the critical understanding of the historian. It is the historian who decides truth about the past on the basis of the critical interrogation of testimony. Like judges who use their experience to determine the veracity of witnesses, historians build up a body of interpretive technique to weed out the compelling from the less compelling. Bradley refines our picture of history by moving history from dependence on testimony to interpretation, and by his consequent realization that the cutting edge of interpretation is provided by the critical activities of historians themselves. This insight into historical method brings it to the edge of one of Collingwood's most revolutionary doctrines: the idea that it is only by re-enactment that the historian can understand the past at all. For Bradley sees that re-enacting the thought of a witness to a past event is not only a condition of understanding it, but also of testing it for truth. However, in Collingwood's view, what Bradley does not see is that re-enactment applies as much to the activity witnessed as it does to the witness. What Bradley leaves unseen is the thought that the historian's critical experience, the singling out of the believable from the less believable, is not an identifiable body of knowledge which comes to the historian ready-made as the fundamental principles of natural science come to the scientist. History is autonomous both in its enquiries and its guiding rules and procedures. Moreover, it is only through the experience of being an historian that the principles which inform that experience are grasped, revised and understood.

Another of Collingwood's interlocutors on the subject of history is Michael Oakeshott. Collingwood considered Oakeshott's reflections on history to be masterly. Not only do they vindicate history as an autonomous discipline of thought; they do so in a manner that eliminates any ambiguity about what history is. Oakeshott writes as a philosopher who argues in his major work *Experience and Its Modes*, (1933) that experience comes alive to us as mediations. Philosophy, science, practice, history and poetry are distinct forms of understanding, each with its own set of postulates and procedures. Oakeshott argues that history is not the course of past events, nor is it the past recollected in the shape of memory. Nor again is the past the practical past, the past to which we may be patriotically attached or romantically wish to emulate. History is separate from science, practice and art. The historical past is a world of ideas in which the historian on the basis of present evidence gives an account of the past as past, of the past for its own sake. What concerns the historian is not past events or sequences of past events which in some way it is the historian's business to exhume and then explain. For in Oakeshott's picture the traditional distinction between history as the course of past events and history as it is thought by the historian is left far behind. What the historian does is not describe the past at all, but to organize and refine present thinking. The test of coherence in history is not the discovery of the previously unknown, but the revision of the historian's postulates and organizing conditions. The historian, as Collingwood describes the conclusion of Oakeshott's investigations, is 'master in his own house' (IH 155); what we think of as the objectivity of history is no more or less than its autonomy and rules of procedure.

We can safely assume that all this was welcome to Collingwood, since the overriding strategy in Collingwood's defence of historical knowledge is to protect it from inappropriate criteria of understanding. A re-statement of the autonomy of history is an important way of achieving this. However, even though Collingwood is clearly impressed by Oakeshott's account of history, there is one respect in which he believes it to fall short. From Collingwood's standpoint Oakeshott leaves the past in its relation with the present in something of a dilemma. Either the past is wholly remote from the present or it persists in the present in some shape or form. On the first possibility the past is dead and so is unknowable. On the second it is present and knowable, but it is not the past. Oakeshott must avoid this dilemma, but he does not tell us how. Collingwood believed that his own emergent doctrine of the living past removed the dilemma. Later we shall ask if Collingwood was right, but for the moment we should conclude that his treatment of Oakeshott is of a piece with his overall method in dealing with past accounts of history. They are each variously refined versions of Collingwood's own.

Collingwood continues his conversation with his contemporaries in Part IV of *The Idea of History* by including theories of history which differ widely from those he supports. While invaluable as a means to history, advances in scholarship are considered in the same light as philology – neither possesses the critical and imaginative power required by history itself. More significant is Collingwood's obvious dislike of theories of history which confuse historical and natural processes, and which deploy methods from the natural sciences such as classification and law-building to explain them. Thus, Toynbee in England and, to a slightly different extent, Spengler in Germany, despite the vast array of learning and historical detail contained in their works, both treat history as a spectacle and so history's potential as a source of self-knowledge is lost. It is their incapacity to free themselves from positivism which makes such theories regressive. Collingwood, therefore, makes a special point of praising Dilthey's emphasis on the notion of lived experience as a development of the first importance in the emergence of historical thought. History proper does not proceed by understanding actions externally as if they were events. Rather it proceeds by historians getting inside the thought of the agent whose actions they are trying to understand. Empathy with the past is, then, for Dilthey and Collingwood, not a luxury that historians indulge, but a necessity if there is to be genuine historical understanding at all. Collingwood's admiration for Dilthey's insights into the character of human understanding links his work on history proper with the evolving study of hermeneutics. Both sharply distinguish historical and natural processes and both insist that without historians reliving the past by making it their own, history would be impossible (IH 171–5).

The discussion of scientific history in Part IV of *The Idea of History* is arranged on a country-by-country basis. By itself this is little more than a convenient focus and we should not read too much into it. But Part IV concludes with Italy, and this is important: first, because it directs our attention to Croce, and second, because Collingwood sees Croce's grasp of history as so extraordinary that in historiographical terms it is a new beginning. Collingwood wants his readers to see that scientific history, as he and Croce understand it, starts here (IH 190–204).

The examination of Croce's views of history is detailed and incisive. Collingwood begins by analysing Croce's early essay on history of 1893. Is history art or science? Croce's answer is definitive. History cannot be understood on the model of natural science. The business of science is to understand facts by relating them to laws or law-like generalizations. But history does not demonstrate causal connections between events; it narrates, and what it narrates is the story of how a given action has come to be what it is. Thus, like art, history yields knowledge of the individual, but, unlike art, history deals with the real not the imaginary. History has been freed from the paradigm of science, but it remains unsystematic because as an art its subject matter is intuited rather than judged.

The question, then, is how a science of the individual is possible. Croce's thought has reached an impasse. If history is knowledge of the individual then it must be art, but if it is art it lacks the critical capacity of science. So how can history become scientific while retaining its concern with the individual? Collingwood traces Croce's answer to his *Logic* of 1909. Here Croce rejects the traditional distinction between universal and particular judgements, arguing instead that history is a branch of enquiry that fits neither. In history the split between logical and empirical statements has no purchase. Thus, the historical judgement rises above the intuitions of art and at the same time keeps the individual as its object. Historians critically think through the actions of the individuals they aim to understand. Even though Collingwood expressed reservations about Croce's attempt to overcome the gap between nature and history, his influence on Collingwood's project of making history scientific is readily apparent.

By the time of Croce's major work on history in 1915 his vindication of history's autonomy had been almost completed. To be sure, the investigation of the connection between history and freedom remained. It was a topic that interested Collingwood too, but for Croce in 1915 it was the protection of history's identity which was paramount. Thus, in his summing up of Croce's importance, Collingwood singles out his conclusion that all history is contemporary history; contemporary not in the sense of belonging to the same period, but in the much more radical sense of belonging to the self-consciousness of historians themselves. True to his precepts, Collingwood explains the relevance of Croce's thought by reliving it. The historian's interest is not with the past as such, but with the past as it is present in the form of evidence, and evidence is history only insofar as historians make it their own through the exercise of the imagination and critical enquiry.

One of the main elements in our thinking about method in the history of philosophy is the view that the meaning of a text derives from the context in which it is written. Even a revolutionary work depends on the arguments it intends to overthrow. Collingwood's ideas about how the history of philosophy should be studied are heavily involved here, but there is something distinctive in Collingwood's approach which gives the relation between text and context a particular twist. We might think of the context of Collingwood's investigations into the nature of history as deriving from romanticism and positivism. Both are opponents in the contest to say what history is. Neither gets history exactly right and on their own they get it pretty much wrong, but, equally, both have strengths. History in the romantic picture comes alive when historians enter into the mental life of the world they are aiming to comprehend. Sharing and criticizing a past way of life is the essential basis for understanding it. For the positivist, however, the first requirement is objectivity in history which means that historians must stick to the establishment of past facts and not read their own present reactions back into them. Whereas romanticism stresses the role of the imagination in history, the positivist concentrates on verification and the avoidance of subjectivity. It is tempting to understand Collingwood's own theory of history as embracing the truthful elements in each view. Thus, Collingwood urges us to understand historical knowledge as the imaginative reconstruction of the past on the basis of present evidence. But Collingwood is aware that even by combining them, history would still be impossible on these views. So Collingwood draws not on truthful elements in each, but supersedes both in a language of his own. In doing this, Collingwood is not reading ideas back into the past but engaging with it as his doctrine of re-enactment requires. For Collingwood believes that it is only by critically re-enacting past accounts that the historian can make progress at all. Hence, when Collingwood speaks about the imagination he means a great deal more than fancy, and when he speaks about evidence he means a great deal more than simply the facts.

Development

When Collingwood writes about the history of history his broad strategy is to relate it to his own. Each account, whether of the ancient or the medieval world, the Enlightenment, or the notion of scientific history reached in the nineteenth century, is regarded as a stepping stone to Collingwood's present view. Of course, Collingwood pays due attention to the particular intellectual and cultural background of each stage, but we can be sure that it is not this alone that catches his interest. Indeed, if it had been, what Collingwood conveys in his lectures would not be history as he understands it. Collingwood brings past thought about history alive by leading it to his own.

The lectures on history of 1936 published as Parts I to IV of *The Idea of History* point to views of history that extricate history from positivism and views that do not. What the lectures are not, however, is an account of the development of Collingwood's thought on history. They are a history of ideas of history, but not a history of Collingwood's own. Certainly, they are written from a present standpoint, but they are not a history of how that standpoint was reached. The views of history discussed in the lectures are stepping stones to Collingwood's thought, but they are not stepping stones in it. There are a number of reasons for this. First, the 1936 lectures express Collingwood's thinking about history at a relatively advanced stage and so they contain little by way of reference to his earlier thought. Second, *The Idea of History* itself is largely composed of lectures, addresses and essays written at different times and for different purposes, and while these refer to the story of his thought they do so only occasionally.

It is important, however, for students of Collingwood to know something of how his understanding of history developed, even though the best account of this development is not to be found in *The Idea of History* itself. *An Autobiography* (1939) is Collingwood's own account of the history of his thought, including his thought about history. It is also the best. For Collingwood's autobiography is a philosophical and literary *tour de force*. As a narrative it is generally reliable, and it is therefore an essential companion to his major writings, including, of course, *The Idea of History*. In his autobiography Collingwood tells us exactly why history came to be his dominant concern. He tells us why we should think of history as scientific in the sense of a systematic body of knowledge, one which is based upon rational principles and inferred from evidence. Much of Collingwood's life was devoted to the elucidation of what we may think of as history proper. There were periods when progress was slow or non-existent. On other occasions work on different philosophical topics took precedence. Even when in a productive mood, Collingwood often left his written results unpublished and so they do not always overlap with his publications of the time. And yet the preoccupation with history remains.

Collingwood's discovery of the importance of history did not come about by chance. It grew out of his practical experience in archaeology and from his dissatisfaction with realism as a compelling account of human knowledge. Two features of the development of Collingwood's thinking about history are worthy of comment. First, it is remarkable just how much of it had been worked out relatively early in his life, and second, how little of it prior to 1924 found its way into his published writings of the time. In this sense, Collingwood's theory of history is the book that never was. It was, nevertheless, the book that Collingwood very much wanted to write. Here the 1914 to 1918 War was the crucible because Collingwood's revaluation of history asks that we think of history not as remote from the present but as highly relevant to it. Politics and the study of history go hand in hand.

In his autobiography, Collingwood tells us that his doctrine of the living past had been in all essentials worked out by 1920. This doctrine reflects his determination to defend history as a body of knowledge which is in its own terms coherent and systematic. His aim was to explain and elucidate history, much as in the seventeenth century Bacon and Descartes explained and elucidated natural science. From immediately before the First World War to the years following it, Collingwood produced many of his theory of history's characteristic ideas. History concerns not the past, but the past encased in the present in the form of evidence. Evidence becomes evidence not from the permissions of authorities, but from the questioning techniques of historians. Question and answer is effective only if historians conceive of their subject matter as action. Thus, understanding, for example, the Battle of Jutland at the end of May 1916 comes not from testimony alone, but from the capacity of the historian to enter into the thinking of those who fought it, to see the situation from their point of view and to critically review the decisions they made. Anachronism is the ever-present danger here, since to treat a trireme as if it possessed the steerage of a sailing vessel or a sailing vessel as if it had the fire power of a battleship is to see naval history in terms of universal problems, and whatever that is it is not history as Collingwood understands it.

We may think of these insights as concerned with the practice of history. They re-evaluate the methods that historians actually use. And yet, important though Collingwood's new history clearly is, if it had stopped there it would not have meant a revolution in our picture of what historians do. It is Collingwood's attempt to find a philosophical licence for his discoveries that gives them their cutting edge. Doctrines like encapsulation and the logic of question and answer reflect Collingwood's capacity to think against the grain. Both are indispensable to understanding what he says about history. Even so, we should note that only fragments of these doctrines (a number in manuscript, on Collingwood's account in his autobiography, with their formulations more or less complete) appear in the major published works of the time. Neither *Religion and Philosophy* (1916) nor *Ruskin's Philosophy* (1919) reveals anything more than hints on the topic of history, and while history is the subject of substantial treatment in *Speculum Mentis* (1924) it is included primarily as a reflection of the book's overall intellectual strategy rather than as a topic in its own right. With this point acknowledged, it is still useful to spend a little time considering *Speculum Mentis*, since it was written when its author's views on history were to some degree in a state of flux, and we should therefore try to single out the views which helped Collingwood to make progress from those that did not.

Overall, the 1920s were years of regeneration in British philosophy. *Speculum Mentis* looks back to Hegel for its aspiration to map human experience in terms of its constitutive forms. Art, religion, science, history and philosophy are distinct forms of understanding arranged hierarchically, each exhibiting merits, but also defects which are then overcome by their successor. History is an advance upon science, but looks beyond itself to philosophy to overcome its specific deficiencies. Differentiation is, then, essential to Collingwood's method. When we look at the differentia of history we see that history and science differ both in terms of their object and their means of enquiry. But while the autonomy of history is touched on, it remains largely undeveloped with the consequence that much of what Collingwood wanted to say about the independence of history is left unsaid. In *Speculum Mentis* the extrication of history from realism is still far from complete, and so in the logic governing the arrangement of forms the weakness of a world view that conceives its object as historical fact quickly becomes apparent. The aim of history is to understand the past as fact, but the past is inaccessible to us and so history shows itself to be a form of error that looks to philosophy for rectification. Collingwood's account of history in *Speculum Mentis* ends in scepticism. For in thinking of history as one voice overlapping with others, Collingwood does not allow it to speak for itself. While Collingwood does insist that it is not their sources that matter to historians, but the capacity to interrogate and, possibly, outwit them, his whole approach is based on history as a form of experience rather than history looked at from the inside. This makes it difficult to communicate quite what it is that makes history different while remaining, nevertheless, a systematic and stable source of human knowledge. After 1924 Collingwood's thinking about history displays a notable shift. The new focus is on the activities of historians themselves. What matters is not so much history as a feature of a phenomenology of human experience, but history found in the work that historians actually do. In the ten years or so from 1924 Collingwood determined to allow history to speak in its own voice.

What emerges from Collingwood's thinking about history after 1924 is just how hard he found it to get his ideas straight. The switch to history in the sense of what historians do was a step forward, allowing the revolution in the understanding of history to be conducted from the ground up. But while this brings difficulties to the surface it did not always help him to deal with them. One major difficulty concerns the doctrine of the living past. How can the past be sensibly conceived as living in the present when it is dead? The past no longer exists. To treat it as if it does is to turn historians into necromancers. Collingwood's hard work for a solution is found in his Die manuscript of 1928. The 1928 breakthrough did not come about in isolation. In his published work of the time Collingwood does much by way of casting realism aside. In this respect the article that Collingwood wrote in 1927, 'The Limits of Historical Knowledge' (1928), is vitally important, since it points forward to the ideas contained in his mature thought. The year 1928 gave Collingwood the advance he was looking for and the article he wrote in 1927 is its essential forerunner.

Realism, the doctrine that what is known stands independently of our knowledge of it, has the effect of making history impossible. Collingwood's problem is to show how to defeat realism while also ensuring history's autonomy. He solves it through an insight of startling simplicity. It is realism that leads to scepticism about history. Find an alternative to realism and the road is open to an account of history which is non-realist and also alert to history's independence. Collingwood now drops all reference to what really happened, or to the past itself. The notion of historical fact is superseded by historical evidence. Since all evidence is present evidence the notion of the past must also be re-described. The past itself is dead and cannot be brought back to life. What lives is present evidence and what gives life to present evidence is interpretation, the use that historians make of it. No historian can go further than the evidence permits, but a gap remains between the past, unknowable as past, and the evidence of it. What enables the historian to make the connection between the relics of battles and the battles themselves, or between the remains of a way of life and the way of life itself? Given that any sort of realist answer to this question is ruled out, Collingwood's difficulty is readily apparent.

Collingwood's answers are found in the manuscript written in 1928 at Le Martouret, a country house near Die in France. It marks the first appearance of the distinction he was searching for – between history proper and false representations of it. The business of history proper is to do with action, not natural event. There can be no history of the planets except metaphorically, no history of fossils except poetically. Astronomy, geology and botany are not history. What gives history its methodology is also its distinctive field of enquiry. In this sense, what historians think about and how they know it are two sides of the same coin. It is the thought that animates the action that gives historians the raw material they need. And it is only because they can rethink that thought that they can understand it historically. It is not, for example, the utensil itself, but its purpose which concerns the historian. It is not the movement of the knife, but the thought behind it which makes it intelligible. Whether the movement is a thrust, a defensive parry, a stab in the back or the twisting which comes from the desire to cause further pain can be decided only by reference to the intention in each case. There can be no history of stabbings independently of context, since it is context that allows us to distinguish between murders, acts of assassination, personal betrayals – 'Et tu, Brute!' – and, say, unintended deaths. So in a justly famous image Collingwood likens the historian to a detective because it is by relating object to context and action to intention on the basis of evidence that the historian proceeds.

From 1928 Collingwood's philosophy of history takes recognizable shape and in the writings that follow we can trace the evolution of its characteristic doctrines. History is a necessary and universal form of knowledge. It is the job of philosophy to make clear what kind of knowledge and by what principles it operates. In his work in the mid-1930s (some of which appears in *The Idea of History* as Part V, Epilegomena), Collingwood brings his idea of a living past to completion. The aim is to separate history from positivism by placing the historian at centre stage. We reach the autonomy of history by grasping what historians do, and what historians do is to understand past thought by present re-enactment. The past is not dead, but encased in the present in the form of evidence. Historians proceed by inferential reasoning to reconstruct the past on the basis of present evidence. By this process of re-enactment history is brought into the closest possible relationship with life, or, to put this in Collingwood's language, it is necessarily linked to self-knowledge. Collingwood expresses these ideas with great subtlety and sophistication in his Inaugural Lecture *The Historical Imagination* (1935) and his Lecture to the British Academy, *Human Nature and Human History* (1936); much of this was intended for inclusion in *The Principles of History*, but even though this was planned and partly written in 1939 it remained unfinished. What it does contain are extended discussions of history in its relation with nature and of the differences between history and biography. Further, Collingwood modifies his earlier arguments regarding the role of rationality in history and also qualifies some of his remarks on the possibility of re-enacting emotions as well as thoughts. If Collingwood's philosophy of history was not brought to fulfilment exactly as he would have wished, this was at least partly because in 1939 he discovered that another work had priority. It was *The New Leviathan* which occupied him in the final years of his life and it is noteworthy that here philosophy retains its independent voice.

Collingwood's idea of history: structural features

Collingwood's reflections on history are characterized by a number of readily identifiable features, since his philosophical style is uniquely his own and deploys concepts which he devised and which have shaped subsequent discussion. Re-enactment (IH Part V, 4), encapsulation (A 97–9) and the inside/outside distinction (IH 213f.) have each been the focus of debate and criticism, as well as the more traditional topics in the philosophy of history on which Collingwood comments, such as causation, objectivity and the nature of historical truth. Collingwood's thought on history overlaps with the philosophy of action because the difference between an action and an event, the nature of motive and intention and the sense in which we can think of actions, both present and past, as caused, are central to both. Equally important is the fact that Collingwood's thought on history ranges widely over questions concerning the historical past, historical method, the historical imagination and knowledge in history. To bring this chapter to a close and to point forward to the philosophical dialogue with Collingwood in the pages that follow I will single out a number of broad topics in which Collingwood's hallmark and the problems it generates are quite transparent.

The possibility of history and the study of history

Collingwood clearly thought that history was a peculiar business. Historians try to write intelligently about states of affairs which no longer exist. They are beyond observation, experiment and reproduction, and yet the histories of these states of affairs, often very different from our own, such as pyramid building, child sacrifice, coming-of-age rituals, as well as others with which we are familiar, such as coronations, strikes, wars, revolutions and marriages, tell us how we have come to be what we are. If history is more than a repository of fact then it involves a conception of knowledge far beyond that of realism. What, then, makes this knowledge intelligible? What makes history possible if it does not conform to the model of science? What gives history its title to exist? It is tempting to think that Collingwood's philosophical answers to these questions also give us what we need to study history. But here we have to be careful. Collingwood says that all history is the history of thought. The intelligibility of history depends on historical re-enactment. Re-enactment is possible only if actions are construed as embodying thoughts. But human actions are often inspired as much by emotion as by thought. Thus, if it is the thought the action embodies which makes history possible, and if what makes history possible also delineates its study, then the field of human history is going to be correspondingly narrowed. But we may be reasonably sure that no historian, except, possibly, an intellectual historian or an historian of science, is going to be content with this. Imagine the history of a battle with the emotions left out. Nothing about the tactical courage (or otherwise) of the commanding officer who plans it, or the stubbornness, say, of the troops who fight it. Would we be able even to understand a battle described in this way? If, however, we take the opposite route and separate questions of possibility from questions of study, the historian's independence is protected. The philosopher is solely concerned with what makes history possible; and, in Collingwood's view, neither sensation nor emotion is able to achieve this. In other words, a work of history may quite legitimately speak of the feelings of the individuals whose conduct it is trying to explain, just as a work of art may contain craft-like characteristics. But just as the craft-like characteristics do not make it a work of art, so it is not the feelings which make it a work of history. Anything that can be called history at all, whatever else it contains, must contain thought. History is made possible by thought, as art is made possible by the expression of the emotions of the artist.

The charge of historicism

Collingwood's thought about history has sometimes been associated with the claim that history finally encompasses philosophy. The first editor of *The Idea of History*, T. M. Knox, if he wasn't also the first to put this view forward, certainly made it current by the emphasis he places on it in the Preface to his edition. For Knox, Collingwood's thought was at its most acute when philosophical questions were kept firmly separate from historical ones, as they were in *Speculum Mentis* (1924) and *An Essay on Philosophical Method* (1933), but by 1936 or so, under the influence of the doctrine that all thought is in an identifiable sense historical, a radical scepticism invades his thinking and philosophy lapses into second place behind history. There are broadly two sets of questions here. The first is exegetical and concerns the textual evidence for Knox's view. In this category also comes the status of works which follow the alleged conversion to historicism, like *The New Leviathan* in which philosophy nevertheless plays an independent role. In addition, we may like to consider the role of philosophy in *The Principles of Art* (1938) because there is no doubt of its primacy in the way Collingwood conducts his investigations in that book by distinguishing art from false versions of it and by analysing the relations between art and language and language and expression. The second kind of question is more interestingly philosophical. Can we sensibly conceive Collingwood understanding history in the way that he does without philosophy remaining separate? For, surely, without philosophy speaking in its own voice Collingwood would not have been able to explore and then identify what gives history its unique character. In his later writings Collingwood is at great pains to stress the historical nature of human experience and to remind his readers that often what they think universal in human nature is, in fact, specific to time and place. But, even with full acknowledgement of this tendency in Collingwood's thought, it still falls well short of a justification for the displacement of philosophy by history. For varieties of human experience remain varieties of something and it is this something which history cannot explain without philosophy stepping in. It was this omission in history which Collingwood tried to rectify in his discussion of civilization and barbarism in *The New Leviathan*. We can see clearly that this issue lies at the centre of Collingwood's thinking. Historicism arises in discussions of *The Idea of History* not because Collingwood's thought is historicist, but because there are times when it sails very close to it. In other words, the problematic relation between history and philosophy is one of the structural features of Collingwood's thought. He could not have reached the conclusions he did in his thinking about history without this becoming an issue.

Historical understanding and relativism

The charge of relativism, like that of historicism, comes about not because Collingwood is a relativist, but because his account of history is easily misunderstood. The criticism is that in his campaign to overthrow realism Collingwood goes too far, so leaving historians completely to their own devices. If it is the historian who occupies centre stage rather than past facts, then there is nothing to arbitrate between conflicting historical accounts except another one. Objectivity in history vanishes. But this, surely, is precisely not what Collingwood is saying. Collingwood gives no licence to historians to say anything at all about the past. First, imagining a past event – say, the exile of Napoleon on St Helena – is based on evidence, and so is totally unlike imagining fairies at the bottom of the historian's garden. Second, re-enacting Napoleon's exile has its own criteria of intelligibility. Thus, whereas it might make sense to speak of an anthropologist going native by behaving like a member of the tribe she is trying to understand, namely speaking their language, engaging in their rituals and so on, it would make no sense at all to speak of the historian re-enacting Napoleon's exile by becoming Napoleon himself. For this, and, as we shall see when we come to debate the criticisms of Collingwood's views, many other reasons, Collingwood's so-called relativism is interesting not because he is a relativist, but because relativism is one of the structural fault lines that cross his thought.

CHAPTER TWO

Collingwood's great discovery: The autonomy of history

Realism

Understanding in philosophy often consists in getting to grips with the 'isms' a philosopher argues against, and of all the 'isms' Collingwood argues against, realism ranks high. He considers it false as an account of human knowledge, dangerously false as an account of moral and political life, and stubbornly and obtusely false in the case of history. We can readily believe that as an ex-realist himself Collingwood knew what he was talking about. Insight into the importance of history came early, but his realist leanings thwarted what he wanted to say. Once Collingwood saw that it was impossible to express his emerging thoughts about history in terms derived from realism, the need to overthrow it became irresistible.

While the sins of realism are identified in *The Idea of History* it is outside that text, in *An Autobiography* (1939), in which the errors of realism are most savagely placed on display. Collingwood believed that realism was false as an epistemology and as an account of historical knowledge. It is now time to discover why. As an explanation of low-grade thinking realism works. 'This is a paintbrush' or 'There are six cars parked in that street', but in cases where the questioning character of knowledge is essential to its achievement, realism scarcely touches the surface. Imagine a detective attempting to solve a serious crime. From the bald facts which face him – the body in the bath, the missing jewellery, the testimony of witnesses – he moves slowly from stage to investigative stage, gradually building up his knowledge of the event. Some leads turn out to be false, new information is disclosed, the crime becomes less mysterious until the detective has a name, and so on. Here knowledge comes not from assertions about objects, but from asking the right questions in the right order. Formulating different questions from new and possibly surprising answers is essential for progress because it is the determining factor in how the next set of answers is reached. Imagine an artist who is unclear about how to express his feelings visually. Some of the art has been successful, but he has reached the point where the painting is stuck. He tries a certain brush stroke. The effect is wrong. Another: now that's *exactly* what I want! What realism ignores in both examples, therefore, is the creative aspect of knowledge. Human beings are world creating, not simply world perceiving, apprehending or observing.

Narrowing knowledge to the point of travesty is not realism's only fault. Collingwood also accuses realism of a logical howler (A 44). Realism claims that what is known is unaffected by being known. This requires that we can compare what is known when it is not affected by our knowledge of it with what it is when it is affected. For without comparison it would be impossible for realism to make its case. You need to compare what x is like plus y with what x is like minus y to show that it makes no difference to x. But, as Collingwood lethally points out, the necessity of comparison proves completely disabling. The realist argument began by denying that what is known is affected by our knowledge of it, but that is precisely what realism needs to assert if it is to meet the demands of comparison. So either realism is forced to define the problem away by setting comparison aside or it is self-contradictory; it asserts what it previously wanted to deny.

Collingwood's attack on realism derives as much from its

inability to account for historical knowledge as it is by its logical faults. If what is known is external to our knowledge of it then history is significant only as a source of past fact. Descriptions of past facts are not like descriptions of present facts, and yet the realist believes that testimony can stand in when observation does not apply, but history seen on these terms is simply not history, since the historian is not integral to the events he is trying to understand. This is the point that realism is completely unable to appreciate.

Realists will argue that blindness to history does not render their epistemology false. Two tough defensive standpoints remain. Both store up trouble for Collingwood's attempt to explain history on non-realist lines. First, the realist insistence that what is known is independent of our knowledge of it does convey our sense that something is going on in, say, the discovery of the right move in a chess game or of the geological composition of the rocks on Mars other than the efforts of the discoverer. There is, in other words, something which exists independently to be discovered. This is important because it counters obvious doubts about discoverers being the sole authenticators of their discoveries. Collingwood may well have a strong case in saying that, except by luck, no scientific breakthrough can be made or unyielding criminal inquiry cracked unless the right questions are asked, but questions are asked of something, and when the right answer is finally reached this answer has to be one that can be appraised by others. Here is realism's second tough redoubt. Knowledge requires checks; and checks point to something existing independently of the checker, some measure of accuracy or objectivity which does not derive from the questioner alone. Knowledge claims depend on a realm of inspection which includes checking for mistakes, authenticity, reliability, replication and many other different kinds of test. The realist position is a conceptual one. It belongs to our understanding of what it is to discover something that something is there to be discovered. Similarly, it belongs to our understanding of what it is to check that something is the case that there exist criteria independent of the checker.

Do these realist arguments counter Collingwood's attack? A realist account of historical knowledge stresses that historical discoveries are no different from any other kind. Without a body of past fact waiting to be ascertained there would be nothing for the historian to discover. Thus, for example, without the previously unnoticed illegitimate daughter there would be no new line of inheritance to interpret, or without the previously undervalued battle there would be no new and possibly revisionary interpretation to be formulated. Knowledge claims in history cannot be checked unless there exists something independent of the checker. The historian cannot be judge and jury in his own case, and we should notice how realist commitments to an independently existing past are deepened as a result.

For the realist it is the past as an independent realm of fact awaiting description and open to verification which blocks historical relativism. There would be little point in thinking about historical discoveries as discoveries unless there was something there to be discovered. An historical fact exists independently of the historian's knowledge of it. From this it follows that an historical fact conveys the past as it actually was. Uncovering new information about family life in seventeenth-century France, for example, would have little purpose unless it was thought to report family life as it was lived. Like the gold awaiting discovery by the prospector or the phenomenon the attentions of the scientist, the past awaits the explanations of the historian.

Little of this impresses Collingwood. What is important about the past, Collingwood argues, is not that it is independent of the knower, but that it is dead. The empiricist model of knowledge acquisition simply does not apply. Given that the past no longer exists, direct knowledge of past fact is impossible. Evidence of what once existed in the form of testimony provides not knowledge but belief, since testimony can only be taken on trust. Certainly, criticism of authorities would provide knowledge, but on the realist account criticism proceeds by reference to fact and past fact is no help here. Collingwood's rejection of realism is important because it provides him with the starting point for his own theory. The notion that a real past exists independently of the historian in the same way as a real present exists independently of present knowledge leads only to scepticism. In Collingwood's view, historical facts are significant only as answers to questions. They are relevant to historians only insofar as they make them their own. And, yet, we should surely accept that one of the strengths of realism is its recognition that relativism won't do. Clearly, this is one of the difficulties which Collingwood's positive philosophy of history will need to address, but for the moment we should notice how an aphorism from 1924 frames the anti-realism of *The Idea of History*. 'Information,' Collingwood writes, 'may be the body of knowledge, but questioning is its soul' (SM 78). Questioning is at the heart of knowledge whether it is the questioning of the scientist probing the structure of atomic energy, the artist contemplating the next brush stroke on the canvas or the historian scanning a past event. The role of questioning in history raises the nature of its methodology – is it art or science? It is Collingwood's views on this topic which will concern us next.

History – is it art or science?

Avoidable dualisms usually offer Collingwood a challenge he is rarely able to turn down, and so we should not be surprised to discover that he thinks of history as neither an art nor a science in the naturalistic sense, but a science nevertheless. Explaining why Collingwood thinks this involves, in part, explaining why he does not think of it as an art, and, in part, why he does not think of it as a natural science. *The Idea of History* is often read as a methodology. Collingwood is seen as telling historians how to do their job. Collingwood's concerns are, however, philosophical. What interests him is not the acquisition of historical knowledge, but what makes history possible at all. His aim is to identify the necessary conditions of historical understanding, and so, as with his procedure in *The Principles of Art* where he separates art from activities which are confused with it, like craft, representation and amusement, history proper is distinguished from understandings which often appear as and in history (note Collingwood's remark at IH 228: 'statistical research is for the historian a good servant but a bad master'), but lack its unique features. As so often with *The Idea of History* Collingwood's meaning is best seen as composite, the result of reflections both inside and outside the text as it was constructed and as it has come down to us.

In what sense, then, does Collingwood consider history a science? In the sense of a body of knowledge which is organized in accordance with its own methods of inference and criteria of truth and falsity, history is a science. However, what determines the organization of historical knowledge is not what determines the organization of knowledge in such sciences as meteorology or chemistry. The meteorologist is concerned to understand events as they happen, to observe them and to build up a body of data which can serve as a basis for universal laws, or law-like generalizations. The chemist is similarly concerned, but proceeds not by observation only, but also by reproducing the behaviour of phenomena through experiments conducted under controlled conditions. However, the historian does not obtain knowledge by observation because the past, unlike the clouds racing across the meteorologist's computer screen, is not there to be observed. Similarly, the historian does not reach understanding by experiment because the past, unlike the protons flying round the scientist's collider, is not there to be experimented on. Moreover, knowledge of the behaviour of one hurricane is conditioned by knowledge of others, just as knowledge of the behaviour of one atom is conditioned by that of others. The scientist, therefore, searches for feature recurrence and stability. In this respect, the starting points of enquiry in science are the assumptions necessary to solve the problem and when the problem is solved the conclusions are universally applicable to the phenomena involved. Whereas the scientist aims for understanding which is entirely abstract, this will not do for the historian. Historical understanding concerns past actions that are closed to explanation as types or instances of laws or generalizations. Thus, the temper of Queen Elizabeth I, the stamping of her foot at pusillanimous courtiers, the cries of rage at foreign diplomats, is unique to her. Certainly, for Collingwood, human actions take place in contexts, and reference to context is often necessary to understand and get a feel for what is going on, but the relation between action and context is not like the relation between the instance and the law which governs it. Whereas the behaviour of the individual electron could be replaced by any other of the same type, the temper of Queen Elizabeth is her own. It is this thought which lies behind Collingwood's rejection of pseudo-sciences, such as sociology or psychology. They are neither science proper nor history proper and so the understanding they offer does not work.

Does Collingwood's separation of history from natural science mean that there is no certainty in history? The certainty appropriate to history, whether understood as the past or as the historian's knowledge of it, is bound up with the characteristics that are special to each. Collingwood is close to Aristotle here. There is little point in asking one form of understanding to follow criteria of exactness and relevance which do not belong to it. Whereas in the exact sciences logical or causal relations determine how subject matter is arranged, in history actions and events follow each other in time. Collingwood argues that the knowledge that there is a date and a place to actions and events is something that the historian cannot sensibly doubt. Equally important is Collingwood's argument that historical understanding proceeds by inference. The logic of historical explanation is neither deductive nor inductive, but it involves a procedure nevertheless, one which leads to conclusions. Thus, Collingwood defends history as a special science that has as its object the understanding of past actions and events through inference and the exercise of the historian's imagination.

The imagination of the historian is not that of the scientist or the artist. Scientists imagine possible worlds and historians imagine how the past must have been, but in neither is the imagination unconstrained as it is in art. Speculation in science is disciplined by the need to conform to scientific tests and procedures. In history there are no equivalent tests and procedures, so what constrains the historical imagination is not fact as the scientist understands it but the availability of evidence and the soundness of the inferences which historians draw from it. Notice that we do find a role for truth and falsity in art. We speak, for example, of a painting or a novel being true to what it portrays or to what it is about. But we speak in this way without requiring the work of art to correspond with a world beyond itself or to represent a reality which is not part of its nature. Collingwood does not argue for rigid distinctions between art, history and science – the presence of imagination in each soon makes us realize that – but he defends history's autonomy nevertheless. And Collingwood's anti-realism eliminates any possibility that the imagining of past ways of life – the fifth-century Greek polis, for example, or village life in twelfth-century Scandinavia – can sensibly be monitored by reference to independently existing ready-made facts about them. Yet, we can be sure that Collingwood understands historical investigation to be a rational and, hence, a checkable process, one in which intuitions are certainly capable of sparking new lines of enquiry, but which are also well short of being lines of enquiry themselves. Collingwood wishes a revolution in history as radical as the seventeenth-century revolution in mathematics and science, but this would achieve little without respecting the particular standards of precision that statements about the past involve. Our next topic takes us to the crux of the matter. Collingwood's great discovery is that history is autonomous. History is not science and it is not art, so what then does Collingwood tell us it is? History's autonomy is established by answering the question: What makes history possible? It is to this that we will now turn.

The autonomy of history

Nothing threatens the autonomy of history more than the belief that a fixed and permanent human nature exists over time, one that is known by analogy with the principles and methods of the natural sciences. To cope with this threat Collingwood devotes much of his 1936 British Academy Lecture on *Human Nature and Human History*, (reprinted in *The Idea of History* as Section Vi, 205–31) to developing his counter arguments and clarifying his own position. Collingwood attacks the idea of a science of human nature by rejecting its guiding assumption that human conduct can be understood in the same way as natural phenomena. Once it is understood that the processes of history are different from the processes of nature then at least one challenge to the autonomy of history can be dismissed. A science of human nature aims to discover uniformities in human behaviour over time and to express these in terms of laws or empirical generalizations, but Collingwood argues that this aspiration for history fails and the cause of its failure is conceptual. Explanation in history is not a matter of establishing relationships between perceived facts, but of treating facts as thoughts which have to be grasped and understood. Thus, once the reasons for, say, Lenin's ascendancy in revolutionary Russia are understood, nothing is to be gained by relating this historical circumstance to any similar one. Far from it being the case that knowledge of the individual depends on knowledge of the generalization, the reverse is true. It is the science of human nature that depends on history.

Collingwood reaches the same conclusion when he dissects the notion of a science of human nature as more moderately formulated. Sometimes a science of human nature is divided into two parts, the first establishing the general characteristics of human behaviour in history, the second their particular manifestations in distinct historical periods. Collingwood argues that this division of labour is unsustainable. If the universal part consists of what the human mind is and the particular part what the mind does (the structure of the machine as against its products), then it is simply not possible to make sense of what mind is separately from what it does. A non-functioning machine is intelligible, but a non-functioning human being is not. So, for Collingwood, if we were able to conceive of the human mind as dormant of any activity whatsoever, we would not be able to study it. Once again it is historical understanding that is prior. Not only does a science of human nature fail, it finds itself dependent on the history it aims to overthrow.

To these criticisms of the project to replace history with science Collingwood adds two more. First, any explanation in science will search for prediction in addition to the establishment of fact, but Collingwood argues strongly that the future is not the historian's concern, 'the historian has no gift of prophecy' (IH 220). The past is unalterable; the future, that which is about to happen, however distant that is from the present, is in principle alterable. History's proper domain is with how the present has come to be what it is. How the present changes and in what directions are the domain of practice. As we shall see, history has important lessons for practice, but Collingwood insists that these will not be learned unless the two areas are kept distinct. Second, Collingwood alerts us to an important sense in which natural and historical processes differ. Whereas in a natural process the past dies in being replaced by the present, in historical processes the past survives in the present. The difference is vital. So to think of human history as, for example, an evolutionary process is to commit a double mistake. First, it confuses human action with natural phenomena, and second, it is blind to the notion of the past living in the present. Given that Collingwood distinguishes the human from the natural and defends the idea of a living past it is not difficult to see how far removed his thought about history is from a science of human nature.

Collingwood's positive views on the nature of history stem from his distinction between natural and historical processes. Both are processes that we can have knowledge of, even though what this involves is different in each case. Thus, when Collingwood identifies the subject matter of history, as he does in *The Idea of History*, he is doing more than simply specifying a field of interest, say, medieval Germany or the origins of the Thirty Years War. He is telling us how it is possible to speak of historical knowledge at all. But Collingwood tells us that knowledge in history is not that of common sense or science. By what title, then, is it to be counted as knowledge? Consider an historian who claims that in May 1917 David Lloyd George had a secret meeting with a representative of the German Kaiser to discuss ending the war. Clearly, our first move would be to ask for proof of some kind. But proof in history is not like proof in common sense or in science. If in ordinary life it is claimed that my neighbour plans to buy my house, I can easily imagine ways of showing this to be true or false. In science, if it is claimed that an experiment successfully demonstrates cold fusion, it can be tested by replication and so shown to be sound or not. But in history, neither procedure is available, so in what sense can statements about the past provide knowledge of it?

Once again, Collingwood's answer alerts us to the autonomy of history. Freeing history from the methods of natural science is the first step in discovering what kind of knowledge it involves. Similarly, freeing history from dependence on authorities is equally essential if the historian is to know what his sources are unable to tell him. Thus, to speak of historical knowledge as opposed to belief in testimony is to construe the activity of the historian as critical. Patching together accounts of the past based on what authorities say about it is mere information gathering. Historical knowledge, as Collingwood understands it, comes from rigorous interrogation of the evidence and the inferences that are drawn from it. Given that direct knowledge of the past is unavailable this emphasis on inferential knowledge is scarcely surprising; and, we should add, inferential knowledge does work. A claim that Lloyd George secretly planned a negotiated peace could be tested either by showing that there was no evidence to support it, or that there was evidence but unwarranted inferences were drawn from it. A warranted inference is, therefore, one of the critical techniques which make up history proper.

There is a well-known view in philosophy that the meaning of a statement is determined by the manner of its verification. Empirical statements can be shown to be true or false. A statement about the past – say, 'Lloyd George secretly planned a negotiated peace with Germany' – looks like an empirical statement, but it cannot be verified like one. Collingwood shows how statements about the past while not being verifiable in any strict sense are nevertheless knowledge conveying. History's autonomy consists of this distinctive epistemology, but it is also characterized by a specific understanding of the object to be explained. Questions to do with method are not far away from questions to do with the possible objects of historical study.

History and human purpose

Collingwood draws a sharp distinction between natural and historical processes. It is not the mechanics of muscle expansion and contraction that explain the assassin's action in striking the emperor dead, but his motive for doing so. Both natural and historical processes exhibit change, but Collingwood argues that the mere fact of change is not sufficient to generate history. So when we picture the archaeologist uncovering past ways of life as a geologist arranges his strata in a chronological series, we are not actually comparing like with like. What concerns the geologist is the classification of types, but what concerns the historian is not type but purpose. It is confusion between these two activities that gives rise to what Collingwood calls pseudo-history (A 109). The material of pseudo-history is no different from that of history proper; it is the past remaining in the present in the form of relics such as pots, documents, books and a huge variety of material objects, including bits and pieces of all sorts. But whereas history proper treats each individual item as evidence by asking for its purpose, pseudo-history asks merely which category it belongs to and in which time period it is found.

Now there are two obvious problems here. Both stem from Collingwood's determination to separate history from nature. First, in history human purposes cannot be wholly divorced from the natural environment that surrounds them. It may well be the case that understanding human conduct requires that we see the purposes it is meant to serve. But what is a perfectly intelligible claim in the philosophy of action looks very different in the context of a philosophy of history because its effect is to narrow the field of history, possibly to make it more of an intellectual matter than it is or can be. For example, we can take Collingwood as saying that it is impossible to grasp the naval tactics at the Battle of Jutland without understanding the plans of the commanders of each side. But, equally, the historian will say that it is also necessary to understand the ship construction of the fleets, the gunnery expertise of the two navies, and also the tide and weather conditions present at the time. Now Collingwood is certain that there can be no history of the weather. Neither can there be a history of tides, even though tidal changes over time can be listed and ordered. Collingwood argues that all history is human history, but human history, as the historian will need no reminding, takes place in sight of nature, and nature, if Collingwood is right, has no place in history. The inside/ outside theory is Collingwood's attempt to solve this problem.

The inside/outside theory

What Collingwood means by the inside and outside of an event is contentious. By the outside of an event is meant its material constitution or its physical movement. By the inside is meant something which can only be described in terms of thought. Put movement and material constitution together with the thought and Collingwood describes the result as action: 'an action is the unity of the outside and the inside of an event' (IH 213). Historical understanding concerns action, in other words, both the outside and the inside of events, but it is clearly the thought which animates the event that is primary. Thus, to take Collingwood's own example (IH 213), Caesar's blood spilling across the floor of the Senate interests the historian only as the visible expression of his assassination. The blood spilling may be understood as following natural laws and, hence, be open to scientific explanation, but take away the constitutional dispute that led to Caesar's death and the result is no historical understanding at all. Similarly, the weather conditions at the Battle of Jutland are relevant only to the extent that they were thought so by the commanders at the time. Take away the thought and the result is the same.

Now on one interpretation the inside/outside doctrine pictures thoughts as inhabiting bodies as inner mechanisms inhabit an outer shell. We might regard this stress on the mental content of events as a function of Collingwood's idealism. It is then not difficult to see the inside/outside doctrine as postulating an inner world as opposed to a publicly observable outside. It is true that Collingwood's way of speaking – the inside and outside of events – does encourage this, as also does the language he uses in *The Principles of Art* (PA 139) where he speaks of a musical composition as a tune in the composer's head. We would be right to find this view strange, since speaking about thoughts as purely private entities which go on inside people's heads would in the case of art ignore everything that is important about it. But this is not the view that Collingwood holds. By 'inside' Collingwood does not mean private, and by 'outside' he does not mean public. What Collingwood repeatedly stresses is the necessity of the medium to understanding in art. Absent a medium of expression, artistic creativity would be simply unintelligible. Artists express what they want to express by actually working on something – the sculpture, the painting, the words in the poem and so on. The composer works on the notes in order to create the tune he wants. Similarly, listeners in the concert hall do not hear the music as brute noise; nor do they merely passively absorb it. They use their imaginations to reconstruct in their minds the process which led to the composition they are listening to. In other words, if we place artistic effort side by side with the work the effort is directed towards then Collingwood's understanding of art as activity becomes clear.

Just as an effort of thought is required in artistic appreciation, so is it also, in spite of the many differences between them, in history. Historical reconstruction, too, asks for the historian to enter another's world. This would be impossible if action were treated as event. What distinguishes action is purpose. Purpose is essential both to material objects and human conduct. We understand the brandy glass better by looking at its design rather than the material it is made of. We understand the warship better when we can explain the military purpose it was intended to serve.

Collingwood does not restrict purpose to practical activities. Politics, economics and military operations are each activities we would think of as purposive. Indeed, Collingwood argues that they would not be what they are unless we thought about them in that way. But the notion of purpose involved here is not utilitarian. In

The Idea of History moral conduct is seen as purposive not because it is exclusively consequence-related or end-directed but because it involves the intention to bring actual life closer to the moral ideal. Neither is Collingwood's emphasis on purpose narrowly pragmatic. Theoretical activities like science and philosophy, possibly even history itself, are purposive in the sense of setting themselves problems to solve. Thus, there can be a history of politics, of economics, of warfare, but only if the historian, on the basis of the evidence, can reconstruct the purpose in the politician's mind, the economist's plan or the military commander's strategy. Action which is unfathomable is beyond historical scrutiny. This is not an empirical point. It is not that some particular actions are just inexplicable, although that is often the case. The limits of history arise from history's autonomy, and if exclusions are the price of autonomy then it is a price that Collingwood has to pay. By the same token there can be a history of science or of philosophy, but only if the historian, on the basis of the evidence, can reconstruct the questions which the scientist or philosopher asked and the answers they gave. A history of science or of philosophy is, in effect, a history of scientific or philosophical problems. But a history of art is different, since the artist is only reflexively aware that the problem is solved once the work is complete. For Collingwood there can be no history of artistic problems, only artistic achievements.

Human history

Unlike the scientist whose business is with the external connections between events, the historian understands the internal connection between the action and the thought which prompted it. Thus, the main task of the historian, as Collingwood pictures it, is to reach an understanding of past actions by rethinking the thoughts of the agents who performed them. If all history is human history, then, as Collingwood puts it, 'all history is the history of thought' (IH 215). Collingwood is led to this view by his sharp distinction between natural and historical processes. There are two aspects to his position and we should consider them separately. First, Collingwood may be taken as saying that whereas human beings have a history animals do not. Now we could write a virtual diary of a dog's existence, including its past. On a certain date I was removed from the dog's shelter; on another date I received my first injection; on another I was walked on the common, etc. A chronology of events, however, is not history. Moreover, in the case of animals a chronology of events is all that *is* possible. Memory, even the memory of the dog waiting for its mistress to return, is not history. Collingwood does speak of cats possessing the rudiments of history because washing in kittens is learned, not instinctive behaviour (IH 227). And yet, while a kitten may have a connection with its past through learning from others, this stops well short of history proper. In other words, even if we were to think of some non-human animal species, such as gorillas or dolphins, having the capacity to learn from their past by returning to their feeding areas, this would not be history as human beings understand it. Second, Collingwood may be taken as saying not that human beings have a history and non-human animals do not, but that human beings have a history of their thought, but not a history of their feelings and instincts. Non-reflective human experience is closed to human history. What Collingwood tends to think of as the animal side of human nature – feelings, appetites, desires and, even, more contestably, the emotions – is something which it is not possible to know historically. There can be no history of love, only a history of thought about love; no history of dreams, only a history of dreams as consciously recounted. A history of the feelings is, then, close to being an oxymoron, since, as Collingwood writes in a dramatic passage, 'we shall never know how the flowers smelt in the garden of Epicurus, or how Nietzsche felt the wind in his hair as he walked on the mountains; we cannot relive the triumph of Archimedes or the bitterness of Marius' (IH 296). Later we will ask whether, if this is what history as the history of thought excludes, it is reasonable to consider it human history at all.

What and why

The autonomy of history consists in the subject matter of history and the historian's ways of thought about it. Historical knowledge concerns actions in the past, and actions in the past are understood by grasping the thoughts in the minds of the agents who performed them. But history does not stop when a past action has been satisfactorily identified; it also asks why the action was performed as and when it was. Without the thought the historian could not grasp what was done, and without the reasons for doing it the historian could not grasp why it was done. Moreover, Collingwood adds to this the additional claim that once the thought and the reasons behind it have been understood, nothing further is required. Unlike the scientist who explains one set of facts by connecting it causally with another set, the historian needs nothing beyond what he has already ascertained to be the case. To use Collingwood's own example, once it has been established that Brutus stabbed Caesar and why, nothing further by way of external causation is needed. As Collingwood writes in a remarkable passage, 'After the historian has ascertained the facts, there is no further process of inquiring into their causes. When he knows what happened, he already knows why it happened' (IH 214).

The inclusion of reasons as well as thoughts comes about because Collingwood places a great deal of stress on the purposive nature of the historian's subject matter. A single action may serve different purposes and so it is important for the historian to separate these by delineating the reasons at work in each case. Moreover, rethinking the thought in the agent's mind involves rethinking the process of reasoning which precedes it. Does it follow, therefore, that only sound reasoning can be rethought? Here we have to be careful, since one of the issues at stake is what counts as a sound reason when the historian's criteria of soundness may not be those of the individual whose conduct he is aiming to understand. Collingwood's firm view is that historical knowledge concerns not the facts of a given situation, but the facts as they were conceived by the agent facing it. To picture historical facts, the towering heights and narrow valleys of the Alps before Hannibal crossed them or the severity of the terrain on the western front in 1917 before the Canadians attacked at Vimy Ridge as existing independently of the thoughts of the historical agents concerned is to think of history as realism understands it. What counts as a good reason is bound up with the perspective of the agent. Certainly, reference to a wider social context is necessary for the historian to get a grip on the meaning of the terms involved, but the key is specific. Collingwood's use of his example of the man who is fearful of crossing the mountains because they contain devils (IH 317) is a clear indication of this.

Collingwood understands human conduct to be reflective. Take away the capacity to reflect on what we do and human history would be unintelligible. Thus, human beings conceived exclusively as perceiving and sensing creatures have no history. For Collingwood there is no history of perception, no history of sensation. The Yahoos that are talked about in *The New Leviathan* have no history. To live without history is to live in a permanent present, in the grip of feeling, not thought. Reason frees us from nature, even though Collingwood stops short of saying that it is our rational nature that is the source of historical inference. Belief systems are not determined by the facts; it is systems of belief that determine what is to count as a fact. Similarly, what is to count as a reason derives not from a universal rational nature, but from the understandings of agents living at different times adopting different kinds of belief. Both of these views are hard at work in Collingwood's example of the devil fearer. A man refuses to cross the mountains for fear of what the devils living there will do to him. What sense can the historian make of this? None whatsoever, Collingwood tells us, if the historian regards this belief as a superstition. To the devil fearer the dangers of devils in the mountains are as strong a justification for avoiding them as snowstorms, rock falls and wolves are to the rational historian. How an individual thinks about the situation he is in is as much part of the situation as the supposed facts regarding it.

What Collingwood says about the autonomy of history may be taken as confining history. The assumptions he makes about the historian's subject matter, reflection, purpose and the like narrow the historian's scope or field of interest. However, we may be sure that Collingwood is telling us what makes history possible as a source of knowledge rather than laying down the law to historians. Moreover, the characteristics of historical subjects are often seen less as static necessary conditions than aspects of behaviour, the importance of which varies enormously from case to case. Thus, while a sense of purpose is an assumption that a philosophical account of history cannot do without actual end-directed conduct is often experimental in which the purposes are formulated not in advance of activity, but as a part of it.

Re-enactment

Re-enactment is central to Collingwood's account of history and a little later we shall look in detail at what he means by this term and take issue with some of the arguments he uses, but first we need to be clear why he thinks that this concept is necessary. He gives the following explanation: 'If then the historian has no direct or empirical knowledge of his facts, and no transmitted or testimoniary knowledge of them, what must the historian do in order that he may know them?' (IH 282). Collingwood's answer is that 'the historian must re-enact the past in his own mind'. (IH 282). In effect, Collingwood is asking that 'the gulf of time between the historian and his object' (IH 304) be diminished from both sides. In Collingwood's philosophy of history the activity of the historian is central. The historian creates history; not, of course, in the sense of making it up, but through the use of the techniques that give history its autonomy. Since the past is beyond reproduction, historical understanding is necessarily selective. Historians pick out what is important, give emphasis to certain developments rather than others and hold back aspects of the story in order to tell it in a more persuasive form. Historical understanding is also constructive. Historical skills are those of interpolation, inference and narrative. Accounts of the past are built accounts which rely as much on imagination as on logic. Historical understanding is, finally, critical. The historian is no historian if he thinks of himself solely as a spectator at the events he aims to understand. Thus, where a military commander's diaries claim victory at a particular battle the historian will ask: If that was the case, why was it not followed up? Or the historian might ask why, if the battle was stalemated, did the commander persist in throwing more troops into it? Once again we see one of Collingwood's fundamental principles at work. What purpose, given the thoughts and circumstances of the time, could such a decision have served? We know that the commander's strategy was to aim for a breakthrough. Did he then change his mind and follow a policy of attrition? Description alone will not answer such questions; criticism – re-enacting the battle from the commander's point of view – just might.

Inference

Historical knowledge, as Collingwood understands it, is wholly different from the past empirically apprehended. The past is not observable. It is remembered, but memory is not history, and so Collingwood needs a form of apprehension which is indirect but at the same time knowledge producing. History and memory part company because history can enlighten us when memory fails or when there is nothing to remember because no one at the time was aware of what happened. Historical inference is Collingwood's solution to this problem. We can be sure that historical inference is neither deductive nor inductive. It follows neither mathematics nor the empirical sciences. And, yet, Collingwood does believe that inferential knowledge is compelling. Inference in history moves not from premise to conclusion, but from evidence to narrative. Evidence, both literary and non-literary, is always present evidence. And present evidence is of the past encased in the present. A history which relies solely on what authorities say occurred in the past is no history at all. It is, as Collingwood remarks disparagingly, mere scissors and paste, a gluing together of accounts taken on trust rather than a critical engagement with the evidence. Evidence, as Collingwood states repeatedly, would not be evidence if it was treated as ready-made. What interests the historian is not the evidence as such, but the inferences that may be drawn from it. The idea is to make use of hypothetical reasoning to establish categorical conclusions. Historical inference is, therefore, a stage-by-stage process, one that is closely linked to Collingwood's logic of question and answer.

In any excavation of a Roman fort, say, or in the examination of the timbers of a trireme found on the bed of the Aegean Sea, inference is hard at work. So it is also, for example, in the reconstruction of the origins of the English Civil War because a mere reproduction of the sources will not provide the narrative the historian wants. Where inference in science moves from particular to universal, in history, by contrast, the object is individual and temporally located. Inference in history proceeds not from data given in advance, but from secure answers to productive questions. Collingwood sometimes speaks of inference as allowing the historian to move beyond his authorities; but if all authorities are open to questioning, inference plays a much more fundamental role. The historical re-enactment of past thought which is essential to history proper depends on inferences drawn from present evidence. Without evidence inferentially understood, re-enactment would turn into something wholly unhistorical, say, imitation or hero-worship.

History and imagination

If inference encourages Collingwood's view of history towards science then imagination moves it towards art. Collingwood argues that most theories of knowledge – knowledge as acquisition, description or correspondence – make history impossible because they neglect the work of the imagination in the way the world comes to be known. Imagining what we do not actually see allows us to construct possible worlds and, hence, to understand our own world better. Imagination allows us to visualize states of affairs as different from what they are. The historical imagination is central to history, but not in quite the same way as it is to knowledge in general. What is imagined need not be wholly fanciful. It may be something as hard-nosed as pondering the cause of my car engine failing. Similarly, imagining the consequences had a decision been taken differently need not be arbitrary because it is counter-factual. What distinguishes the historical imagination specifically is its concern with the past, and since the past exists in the form of present evidence the historian can imagine nothing that is not permitted by the evidence. This is one of the differences between the historian and the historical novelist. Even so, it is not that a capacity to imagine the past is an ability which is merely useful to historians. For Collingwood, an unimaginative historian is something like a contradiction in terms.

Towards the close of his Inaugural Lecture (the main source for much of Collingwood's treatment of the role of imagination in history, reprinted in IH 231–49), Collingwood borders on making imagination the touchstone of history proper. His route to this conclusion starts with the separation of history from testimony and moves to the realization that it is the imagination that enables the historian to fill in the gaps between his authorities. But then

Collingwood forces us to admit that what are considered author-ities in history are no more (or less) than functions of the historical intelligence itself. To picture the historian's authorities as given data around which the imagination does its work is to picture them empirically and, as Collingwood argues repeatedly, there is no room for empirical fact in history. It is therefore the historical imagination which constitutes history proper. Take imagination away from history and nothing is left except a flat record of events. Collingwood clearly wants this conclusion, but reaching it gives him a problem. If the historical past is a constructed past and a constructed past is essentially an imagined one, what is the difference between a novel about the past and a history of it?

Collingwood's solution hinges on differences between art and history. Imagining is not an incidental gift in art or history. Collingwood argues (to some degree following Kant) that the imagination operates a priori, as he puts it: 'we cannot but imagine what cannot but be there' (IH 242). When we perceive the table top we imagine the underside, when we see the unopened parcel we imagine its contents, and so on. In art, by contrast, there are no objects of perception. Here the unrestricted imagination of the artist determines what is seen. In history the a priori imagination is also active, but its object is different. It cannot be an object of perception since the past no longer exists. The historical object is a past thought and the role of the imagination in history is to recon-struct it. It is to show us imaginatively 'what cannot but be there'.

How, then, is a novel about the past different from a history of it? Both are narratives in which events and circumstances combine with character and motivation to produce a compelling tale. Collingwood stresses that each is an independent world, self-justifying and self-explaining. History, however, cannot be self-authenticating. The historian may be his own authority, but this does not authorize him to say anything at all about the past. There are rules of historical method which, if not followed, ensure that the historian's authority quickly dissolves. The reasons Collingwood gives for this are absolutely clear. First, as the object of historical investigation the past has a definite spatial and temporal location. The assassination of Trotsky happened at a specific time in a specific place. The sinking of the battleship Prince of Wales happened at a specific time during the Second World War and at a specific place. Whereas art ranges well beyond mere topographical fact history contains it, not, of course, as fact, but as the historical imagination reconstructs it. Thus, a wholly imagined artistic world – say, that of George Orwell's *Nineteen Eighty-Four* – grips us, even though 1984 has come and gone. Second, whereas fictional accounts of the past differ without disagreeing, the historical imagination must be exercised consistently with other, equally persuasive historical accounts. Whereas there are many fictional worlds there can only be one historical world. Starting with chronological and topographical relations – this stone was in place before that and this stood here rather than there – the single historical world is elucidated progressively in terms of actions and the thoughts which enable the historian to make sense of them, so this policy produced the following effects and this action negated that. Since the imagination in fiction is exercised solely at the novelist's command it does not need the judgement of peers which is essential to history. Third (and most importantly for Collingwood), the exercise of the imagination in history must take place in relation to evidence. We may well find an imagined past compelling because it appeals to our aesthetic or even political instincts, but without a firm embedding in evidence a past so described is not history as Collingwood understands it.

History and self-knowledge

L.P. Hartley famously states, 'the past is a foreign country: they do things differently there', but Collingwood makes strenuous attempts to show that history is a source of self-knowledge. Understanding myself as human, understanding myself as the kind of human being I am and understanding myself as I am and nobody else is, are exercises in historical intelligence. Understanding who I am necessarily involves understanding how I have come to be who I am. With this ambition for history in mind, how might Collingwood have responded to Hartley's view? Feelings of bafflement when we are confronted by photographs of us in our youth or of long-dead family members when they were young are not uncommon. Intuitively, then, Hartley is right, since not only is the past not my country, it is one I would not recognize even if it were possible for me to visit it. Memory contradicts this, but memory is short term and often unreliable, and, much more importantly for Collingwood, it is not history. I do not recognize the thoughts and experiences I have as my own because I can remember earlier thoughts and experiences. Self-recognition is bound up with the effort of understanding my past as mine. Moreover, the knowledge involved in this is not knowledge as realism pictures it. For the realist the object of knowledge is independent of the activity of knowing it. But if my past stands to me as an external object then it is unknowable because my past no longer exists, and if my past no longer exists then I cannot be acquainted with it, and if I cannot be acquainted with it I cannot recognize it as my past as opposed to the past of anyone else.

Collingwood clearly thinks that realism is false as an epistemology and as a philosophy of history, but he does have to acknowledge that the past is relevant to the present only in the form of an ideal. The past is dead. It has vanished beyond recall. So how then can something which no longer exists tell us who we are? If the past is a foreign country, we could conceivably visit it and with some effort come to understand its language and customs. But even though the language and customs of my past are mine and so I should not have any difficulty in understanding them, I cannot revisit it. On the Hartley view, Collingwood's account of history as self-knowledge looks stillborn; how, then, does he rescue it?

We need to be sure of the importance of this question to Collingwood. History and self-knowledge are not connected empirically. Collingwood is not saying that in coming to understand myself a few pieces of information about my past might prove useful. Nor is he saying that history is just one of the routes to self-knowledge, as if it could be acquired in some other way, say, by introspection or from the study of psychology. In fact, Collingwood's classification of psychology as a science of feeling issuing in generalizations about mental states alerts us to the impossibility of this suggestion. Collingwood has to show that history is an essential constituent of self-knowledge. He has to show that in the absence of an understanding of my past I could not understand myself.

Collingwood's first move is modest. Imagine you are experiencing feelings of discomfort. You are unable to settle and feel in some way disturbed and embarrassed, so you ask yourself, Why? Your immediate feelings cannot give you the answer. Attempting to generalize from these feelings to others of the same type gets you nowhere. Looking to your past, however, enables you to reflect that you received a letter that morning which criticized you in unfavourable and wholly justifiable terms. You recognize the connection between your present feelings and the receipt of the letter. That process of recognition, Collingwood says, is 'nothing else than historical knowledge' (IH 174). Now you see yourself differently. You have understood something about yourself that you did not know before. At this point Collingwood raises the stakes. Imagine you are an historian trying to understand some historical figure, say, Julius Caesar. You achieve this by re-enacting in your own mind the thoughts that Caesar had in acting the way he did. Of course, you do not become Caesar; you remain who you are. Even so, your present has changed. It is no longer your immediate present knowable if at all only by private introspection. Neither is it your immediate present knowable by relating it to other present states. Your present is now informed by knowledge of the past. But what, then, does this past informed present consist of? It is not knowledge of the past at the expense of the present and it is not knowledge of the present at the expense of the past. It is, in Collingwood's view, historical knowledge. This is precisely what history is as Collingwood understands it: 'knowledge of the past in the present; the self-knowledge of the historian's own mind as the present revival and reliving of past experiences' (IH 175).

Conclusion

Collingwood's great discovery is that history must be understood as *sui generis*. His achievement is that of making us see why. History is not about the past. History is about the past as reconstructed in the present. Collingwood's paradox – all history is contemporary history – is not unintentional. He wants us to realize that this is the only way of rendering history intelligible while avoiding the twin perils of naturalistic science and romanticism. Two key passages in *The Idea of History* make this aim transparently clear. The first comes from *The Historical Imagination* and it tells us unambiguously that the historian's concern is not with an imagined past but with the past as such. Collingwood writes:

'what the historian thinks about is Elizabeth or Marlborough, the Peloponnesian War or the policy of Ferdinand and Isabella' (IH 233). Theories of knowledge as acquaintance tell us how we see what we see and observe what we observe, but the past is beyond sight and observation and, therefore, realism as applied to history doesn't work. So, for Collingwood, the historian's true object of study must be the past reinstated in the context of the present. Hence, the second key passage in *The Idea of History* where Collingwood writes that 'history, then, is a science, but a science of a special kind. It is a science whose business is to study events not accessible to our observation, and to study these events inferentially, arguing to them from something else which is accessible to our observation, and which the historian calls 'evidence' for the events in which he is interested' (IH 251–2). Collingwood does not believe that his picture of history as autonomous undermines its claim to knowledge. Historical understanding is warranted, first, by its being systematic – it possesses a methodology, that of the logic of question and answer, which determines where the historian hits the mark and also where he is wide of it; second, it is concerned with the human world – the actions of beings whose intentions and purposes can be reconstructed; third, it is open to counter-argument because it derives its account of the past from evidence which can be rationally assessed; and, fourth, it is a body of knowledge from which we can learn. It is, as Collingwood writes, 'self-revelatory' (IH 18).

I have called Collingwood's great discovery an achievement. Like all achievements in philosophy it has been extensively discussed and criticized, often severely. It has not been ignored. In the next chapter we will enter into a conversation with Collingwood and also sharpen the focus a little by examining each of the main components of Collingwood's theory of history in turn. Is history's autonomy authentic? In what sense do historians 're-enact' the past? What exactly is the logic of question and answer? It is to the discussion of these questions and others like them that we now turn.

CHAPTER THREE

Arguing with Collingwood (I)

The problem of re-enactment

If there is one doctrine that makes Collingwood's writings on history stand out it is surely his claim that historians understand the past by re-enacting past thought. What Collingwood says about history does not depend upon re-enactment alone. Evidence, imagination and inference are each heavily involved in what historians do. For the purposes of philosophical discussion, however, re-enactment can be treated separately. It is in any case a complex idea and so it needs unpacking.

Imagining oneself in another's shoes or looking at a decision from another's point of view both require something like a leap of sympathy. Empathy, however, is no less genuine for being intuitive, and whatever else re-enactment is we can be sure that it extends well beyond the past unreflectively understood. Collingwood himself traces the origins of re-enactment to the appreciation of music. An indispensable condition of writing a history of past music is that it can be performed in the present. In attempting to reach back to the past it is the present that is the historian's touchstone. Thus, what applies to past music is also found in past battles, conferences and treaties; in fact, to the whole human past understood as activity rather than event.

Early readers of *The Idea of History* tended to interpret re-enactment as a piece of methodological advice. It is one of the keys to unlocking the past. Understood solely as methodology, however, re-enactment is easily misunderstood, and so later critics interpret it not as a useful tool but as a condition of history itself. Dispense with re-enactment as a method and another mode of explanation may well replace it. But dispense with re-enactment as a condition of history and you have no history at all.

We may think of re-enactment as a load-bearing doctrine. It is the cross-beam upon which the whole structure depends. Weaken the beam and you are left with history as realism understands it. The realist sees history on the spectator model. Since historians cannot witness events that no longer exist they must defer to the accounts of those who did, but at best, Collingwood argues, this delivers belief, not knowledge, since knowledge comes about from historians criticizing their authorities, not merely assenting to them. Moreover, history understood on the spectator model pictures the relation between the historian and the past event as an external one. To embrace a history of human conduct the spectator model has to be dropped completely. Historians are not independent of the past, but internally related to it. So when Collingwood asks on what conditions history is possible he answers by saying that the historian must re-enact past thought in his own mind.

The 'must' here is a logical 'must'; erase re-enactment and whatever is left is not history as Collingwood understands it. To get to grips with re-enactment and why it is important, it is necessary to unpack it. First, we must look at Collingwood's claim that what is re-enacted is past thought. Why thought? Collingwood writes that 'to know another's act of thought involves repeating it for oneself' (IH 288). For Collingwood the act of thought is not solely the thought as it actually happens. Unlike sensation and feeling which belong only to immediate experience, thought is both immediate in the sense that it occurs in the here and now and mediate in the sense that it has the capacity to live again in different contexts. Thought is not simply a private mental event, something that is uniquely accessible to the agent who engages in it. Mental acts as such are neither true nor false, but acts of thought are performed with awareness and deliberation. Moreover, thinking is an activity which can be re-thought. Thus when I think, for example, about my next move in a delicately poised game of chess it is possible

for others to retrace my steps to discover why I made the decision
I did and to debate whether or not it was sound. Thinking, we
might understand Collingwood as saying, is always thinking about
something, a point which might make critics of Collingwood's
idealism sit up. Further, it is thinking about something in a defensible or systematic manner. So grasping what I am thinking when I
make my chess move refers to the context of the game as it stands,
the premises of my strategy and the questions I asked myself
when I examined stage by stage what would happen if I moved
my queen rather than sacrificed a pawn, and so on. Collingwood
thinks of thought, therefore, as something that is intended to
solve a theoretical or practical problem. Even idle thoughts are
never wholly idle and thoughts that I would prefer to avoid do
not for that reason cease to be thoughts. It is, then, not the fact
of my thinking that interests the observer of the chess game, but
the process of argument which led me from one conclusion to the
next. Similarly, it is not my feelings of elation at having won (or
of disappointment at having lost) that the observer re-enacts, but
the reasons for my success or failure. My feelings come when they
come and vanish when they vanish, but my reasons are within my
control and so may be rethought by others wishing to see why I
won or lost.

Thought, Collingwood writes, is 'not private property' (*Outlines
of a Philosophy of History*, 1928, IH 450). Given that it is thought
which the historian re-enacts how does Collingwood see the
relation between the thought and its re-enactment? Framing the
question in this way may be considered slightly misleading because
Collingwood wants to show not that there are two thoughts, but
that the thought and its re-enactment are one and the same. His
ambition for re-enactment can be appreciated from the following
passage: 'the historian of a certain thought must think for himself
that very same thought, not another like it' (A 111). But this
seems to challenge common sense. How can Napoleon's thoughts
on Elba be the same as my re-enactment of them in my twenty-
first-century study? Surely there is not one thought, but two.
Moreover, the second thought cannot be a repeat of the first. And,
yet, Collingwood is insistent. History would not be possible unless
Napoleon's thoughts and my rethinking them are the same.

Collingwood's solution to this problem is to say that it is the
context which separates the thought from its re-enactment. The

thought itself remains the same. But how can it remain the same when it is not Napoleon who thinks it? Consider the following cases. A crime has been committed and the police decide to stage a re-enactment of it in order to jog people's memories, uncover new witnesses and so on. Here the crime is re-enacted, but it is not repeated. Consider next a batsman who plays two identical cover drives off successive deliveries. The shots are the same in every respect except numerically. The timing and execution of the shots are mirror images of each other. Both hit the boundary in the same place. Here we have repetition, but we do not have re-enactment. Collingwood wishes historical re-enactment to be different from both of these. To re-enact a thought is to repeat it. There are not two thoughts, but one operating in different contexts. So to understand Napoleon's thoughts on Elba the historian must repeat them for himself. The repeated thought and the thought it repeats must be the same. That is what re-enactment means.

Collingwood's doctrine seems perverse, so he spends a great deal of time attempting to demolish objections to it. The first objection is absolutely fundamental. Thoughts, the objector states, are no more extendable in time than feelings and sensations. If it is my thought then it is happening to me now, just as my feeling the cold, say, or feeling miserable are experiences which are happening to me now. My immediate experience is closed to re-enactment, once it is over it is beyond recovery; the most we can expect is an experience which is something like it or which resembles it in some way.

Collingwood's counter is to say that the thought/feeling parallel does not work. Not all experience is immediate. Acts of thought do not stand in the same relation to time as sensations and feelings. It may be, for example, that the itch which irritates me comes to me when it comes and not to you and then vanishes in the flow of time, but my recognition of it as an itch is different since it involves processes of thought – say, comparisons between itches and aches – which are not only open to reconstruction by you, but which survive for future generations to reconstruct and reflect upon. Moreover, you would not be able to grasp what it is about the itch that enables me to recognize it without a reconstruction of my thinking which is exact. In other words, it is not sufficient simply to copy the processes of thought which led to the recognition. If it is to be the same thought that is re-enacted then each stage in my process of thinking must be re-enacted as a stage, and each following stage re-enacted in the same way and so on. Any attempt to deny that the two thoughts can never be the same rests on the possibility of comparing them, and comparing them is possible only by reconstructing the original thought to see whether there is a difference and, if so, where it lies.

So far Collingwood has resisted the first objection that no thought can be re-enacted and that no two thoughts are the same. The first objection claims that re-enactment proves too little; the second that it proves too much because in rethinking past thought the historian cannot but rethink it as his own. Historical knowledge derives from present re-enactment, but if the thought that is re-enacted is the same as the historian's own then what the historian knows is never the past but the present. There are, in other words, not two thoughts, one past and one present, but one, the present re-enacted thought; so, the objection runs, although common sense tells us that knowledge of the past is different from knowledge of the present, that, on Collingwood's account, is exactly what historical knowledge turns out to be.

It is important that this objection is overturned and the arguments towards the close of Section 4 are aimed at achieving this (IH 296–302). Collingwood thinks of thinking as reflexive. Thinking and the awareness that we are thinking are two sides of the same coin. When a problem is encountered we retrace our steps to find where our thinking went wrong. We anticipate future difficulties and try to adapt our thinking accordingly. I can compare my struggles in the chess match I am currently playing with previous efforts, with moves in past games that were once successful and with those that were not. However, reflection on past thought is different from reflection on past feelings. In the case of feeling what bridges the gap between the present reflection and its object in the past is memory. Moreover, in order to remember, for example, the anger I once felt, I do not need to re-experience it. Rethinking what occasioned the anger may help me to understand it, but then what I am rethinking is not the feeling but the reason for it. Perhaps some trace of what I once felt may trigger the memory, but neither the trigger nor the memory requires that the feeling be re-enacted. 'I remember that her behaviour made me very angry' is perfectly intelligible without 'It still makes me angry to think about it'. Further, the anger which lingers is not the same as the anger I felt at the time.

Re-enacted thought, however, is different. When a past thought is re-enacted it is revived not as a pale reflection of the original, but as the same. Whereas re-enacted anger turns into anger that is simulated, re-enacted thought is no less authentic than the thought it re-enacts. The direction in which Collingwood is moving could not be clearer. He wants us to see that history does not visualize the past as memory does. In the memory the past is a spectacle, something we might fancy ourselves observing. Unlike the remembered past, the re-enacted past is alive, but it lives only with the present's permission. When I rethink a thought of Plato's, say, it must be the same, but that re-thought thought is also mine, so whose thought am I thinking – Plato's or mine? If it is mine then I know something about myself, but not about Plato. I have reached understanding, but not historical understanding. If it is Plato's then I have knowledge of a past thought, but it is not mine and since Collingwood argues that history depends on my present re-enactment then it is not historical knowledge either. The objection tries to make Collingwood choose between two alternatives – either it is Plato's thought or it is mine. There is no third choice. Critics of Collingwood will say that the ghosts of realism have returned to haunt him. It appears that Collingwood is experiencing difficulties, so how does he deal with them?

Of course, it is the third choice that Collingwood wants, so he argues that there is a respect in which Plato's thought is different from my re-enactment of it and a respect in which it is the same. Plato's thought is different in the sense that his actual experience of thinking it and developing it against the views of his opponents arises in a specific historical context, as obviously does mine. However, Plato's thought is also the same as my re-enactment of it because as a thought and not a feeling it can exist in both contexts: Plato's and mine. Thus, insofar as I can get Plato's thought right, it remains the same thought even if in my re-enactment of it I show how it can be refuted. If thought is wholly context dependent then both thoughts are different. But thought is capable of being rethought beyond its immediate context. Moreover, thoughts are not the same in the sense that, say, pins are the same as other pins or staples are the same as other staples. I make Plato's thought mine in the effort of rethinking it. That is the force of Collingwood's anti-realism. It is also the force of the very important qualification – 'if I can get Plato's thought right'. Sameness does not come to the historian ready-made.

My rethinking of Plato's thought is not simply the same thought repeated. Rather it is only insofar as the historian can re-enact the thought that it can be considered the same.

It is what Collingwood calls the 'copy theory' of knowledge that is his target here. There is no sense in which the re-enacted thought is a copy of the original as one pin is a copy of another one or one staple is a copy of another. Whereas the second pin is a copy of an existing pin the past has no existence at all. Re-enacting the past is, therefore, completely different from copying or, indeed, imitating it. When the historian rethinks Plato's thought he has, not a copy, but Plato's thought exactly. It is the activity of rethinking that Collingwood wants us to appreciate. If Plato's thought was simply passively received then the historian would not understand it. It is the active step-by-step reconstruction of Plato's thought which makes it the historian's own. Resistance to the 'copy theory' is another illustration of Collingwood's determination to separate his thought from realism. So far does Collingwood wish to go in this respect that he sometimes refers to the present re-enactment of past thought as *'the past itself'* (IH 450), insofar as the historian can know it as such.

We should be a little wary here. Collingwood stresses that past thought is not made actual by its being re-enacted. The past remains the past, non-existent, in itself unknowable, an ideal. What is actual is the historian's present re-enactment of the past and it is present re-enactment which provides the basis for the historical past. Once more it is Collingwood's anti-realism that is calling the tune. Re-enacting the battle does not mean actually fighting it any more than not re-enacting it means that no battle took place. The engine room of history is always the present in the form of what may be thought about and what the evidence permits.

Re-enactment, then, is the essential element in all history. Whether it is the historian of mathematics writing a history of differential equations or the constitutional historian writing a history of legal reform, each must reconstruct the situation as it was faced at the time. Knowledge of the past comes not from apprehension since there is no past to apprehend, but from re-enacting past thought on the basis of present evidence. Even so, Collingwood is forced to acknowledge that realism does have strengths. Discovery, the realist will insist, cannot happen twice. The historian rethinking Einstein's famous equation, $E=mc^2$, must retrace the steps which led to it, but Einstein took each step for the first time and so had no steps to retrace. It would appear to follow, then, that on Collingwood's account of history, discoveries, inventions, original ideas, also, possibly, first-time experiences, must remain opaque. A kiss may be just a kiss, but the first kiss is different. As Jonathan Barnes cautions, 'there may be future raptures – but you can't ever recapture the first, fine, careless one' (Jonathan Barnes. (2007), *Truth, etc, Six Lectures on Ancient Logic*, Clarendon Press, Oxford, 42).

The historian's business is to do with human action. Actions are understood in terms of the thoughts of the agents who perform them. Collingwood outlines clearly the conditions of historical understanding. These are, first, that thought must be expressed in language or in an identifiable non-linguistic form of expression, and second, that it must be capable of being rethought by the historian who is aiming to understand it. By drawing these boundaries Collingwood does not turn human history into intellectual history. Human beings are portrayed as problem-solving creatures, but the problems themselves can be as much practical as theoretical. The design of a Minoan burial ground, a classical Indian love ritual, nineteenth-century British electoral reform, female emancipation in communist China, are all possible objects of historical knowledge because each is an expression of thought either in the form of a graspable idea or as a way of dealing with a practical difficulty. However, historical knowledge does not consist in first discovering the thought and then understanding it. That would be to construe thoughts as facts. Thoughts cannot be discovered unless they are understood and they can be understood only by being re-enacted. The historian must think that thought again if the past is to be known at all. It is, in other words, impossible to know the past without re-enacting it. Historical re-enactment is a reworking of a process of thought, drawing the same conclusions, making the same appraisals, considering the same alternatives. There is nothing hypothetical about this. The historian can postulate nothing which was not available to the agent at the time. This is the true impact of Collingwood's insistence that the historian, in re-enacting past thought, re-enacts the same thought and not one that is similar or approximate to it.

The past, then, does not come to us as light from a distant star. Without the historian's critical engagement the past could not come alive at all, but critical engagement with what? If the answer is with decisions as actually arrived at and made, then history is going to be a rather lifeless affair. If, on the other hand, it is with what may have happened as well as what did happen, then Collingwood seems to be giving historians the freedom to say what they like. In fact, Collingwood strikes a persuasive course in addressing these questions. The political historian trying to understand the actions of, say, Lloyd George during the munitions crisis in the First World War will re-enact his intentions and the situation he faced. This will include 'possible ways of dealing with it' (IH 215) as well as the policy he actually followed. Does this make history too conjectural? Not at all, so as long as the alternatives which the historian re-enacts are those that were considered by the agent at the time. But does this mean alternatives that actually were considered or those that could have been considered? Once again Collingwood is permissive. The historian in re-enacting past thought, both theoretical and practical, subjects it to criticism, 'forms his own judgment of its value, corrects whatever errors he can discern in it' (IH 214). It would be a poor sort of historian, Collingwood suggests, who treats the past as immune from revision, even if the revision takes place in the historical imagination and the historical imagination takes place in the present. Re-enactment, in other words, includes counter-factual discussion as well as the delineation of what actually occurred.

Thus, when Collingwood says of the historian 'when he knows what happened, he already knows why it happened' (IH 214), we should not interpret him too restrictively. Historical knowledge concerns why one thing happened, but also why one thing happened as opposed to some other thing. Re-enacting the thought is not the same as establishing the cause of an event. Given that for Collingwood all history is human history and given that human beings commonly look back on their decisions and wonder if they decided rightly, it seems entirely reasonable for Collingwood to include such possibilities in historical discussion. Indeed, counter-factual argument does make sense. One football fan can say to another after the game, 'if the manager had not substituted our winger we would have won'. Lack of intelligibility here sometimes relates to what actually happened – hence the response, 'not really, as we lost 4-0', or to past experience – hence the response, 'he hasn't scored in ten games', or from a reference to other aims and purposes – hence the response, 'true, but he's saving him for the cup tie and he didn't want his leg broken by that thug of a full back'.

So when the historian writes a history of events that did happen such as the race by the German forces to the French coast in the early years of the Second World War it is not unreasonable for him to also discuss the one event that did not happen when they reached it, namely the invasion of England in May 1940. Here counter-factual discussion is relevant. Moreover, this kind of discussion is surely what Collingwood means by critical. Thus, when Guderian's armoured columns were ordered to halt just ten miles short of the French and Belgian beaches it is not unreasonable for the historian to explain the order by reference to Hitler's fear of the possible dangers involved in a mass military transportation across the Channel or his preoccupation with the planned invasion of the Soviet Union. Debating Hitler's reasons for giving the order is not like debating what would have happened had he ordered differently because this concerns an unknowable future, but even so Collingwood's point remains. It is the historian who holds centre stage. Re-enacting the agent's thought means finding and rehearsing the reasons for what he did and, as we have seen, there are cases where finding the reasons means finding possible reasons, but finding possible reasons does not imply that any old reason will do.

However, not all of past life is historically reclaimable. What cannot be re-enacted cannot be known. And what cannot be known, for Collingwood, includes the immediacy of the past, an immediacy that is essential to sensation and to feelings, and which is to some degree present in thought, too. Historical blunders, failures of various kinds, even accidents and strokes of luck can be rethought so long as they can be related to the agent's aims and purposes. Not that Collingwood elucidates purposive action solely in syllogistic terms. The logic of question and answer is especially relevant to human conduct in cases where propositional logic fails or can find no purchase. A gamble, taking a chance or the last throw of the dice may each be intelligible answers to intelligible questions even though unlicensed by practical reason. Thus, whereas the storm in which the ships carrying the ammunition were lost would have had a natural cause, the decision to take the risk in bad weather was a human one and so is open to historical view. Dreams, unconscious warnings and premonitions of triumph or disaster are, however, closed. There can be no 'history of second sight', Collingwood writes (IH 310), since, even though statements which testify to it could be found these would be testimony only and so would not qualify as historical knowledge as Collingwood understands it. The unfathomable cannot be reconstructed and so does not belong to history proper. Similarly, we should not think that Collingwood's picture of history as the history of thought restricts it to the thought of individuals, their particular motives and intentions. The test of purpose applies to collective human institutions, movements and practices. In politics, for example, councils, parliaments, assemblies of various kinds, communes and corporations are decision-making bodies, even if they do not have intentions as do individuals. Moreover, their establishment reflects ideas, possibly in the shape of a worldview.

There is, however, in Collingwood's philosophy generally as much as in his philosophy of history, a fundamental distinction between thought and feeling. It is the immediacy of sensation which closes it to re-enactment. We can in principle rethink the process of thought by which Archimedes reached his famous discovery, but we cannot experience the waters of his bath rising as he did, nor can we experience his feelings of excitement when he realized what it meant. Here it is not only the impossibility of repeating 'Eureka!' which blocks history (see IH 297–8), but the immediacy of the sensations and feelings that surround it.

In denying that the emotions can be re-enacted it is sometimes claimed that Collingwood takes the heat out of history. We have the bones, but not the flesh, the thoughts, but not the passions. Thus it has been argued that this is not going to be a history which will convince anyone. A battle, for example, Trafalgar or Waterloo, is not a purely intellectual affair confined to the strategy in the commanding officer's mind or the charts or maps on the commanding officer's table. It is true that Collingwood does not think of the emotions simply as physical occurrences and he does stress that it is not possible to experience a given emotion without, first, being aware of it, and second, expressing it (PA 282). Furthermore, Collingwood does seem to broaden the scope of re-enactment by suggesting that if a given emotion belongs specifically to a particular action, as fear of failure attends sitting an examination, we can after all find space for the emotions in history (PH ch. 2). None of this, however, makes Collingwood give up his basic point – while Napoleon's thoughts during his exile are open to re-enactment his feelings as he experienced them are not.

Given that people often think long and hard about their own emotions and the emotions of others Collingwood's exclusion clause seems unpersuasive. Moreover, it is a weakness which reveals cracks in the general theory. If re-enactment is a condition of historical knowledge then the historian can never know a past emotion. If, by contrast, re-enactment is a method then the historian is able to imagine what it was like to experience a given emotion in a given situation, but he is not able to re-enact it. Collingwood, however, does not visualize the historical imagination ranging across the past without the discipline of re-enactment. History without the emotions becomes a rather bloodless affair, but with them it ceases to be history at all, or so Collingwood seems to say. It is a problem which we need to consider further.

The problem of imagination in history

For those who understand Collingwood's philosophy of history as an interlocking whole, the historical imagination is neither the foundation of history nor simply one of its constituent parts. Imagining the past without re-enacting it may, if it is well done, take you back to the world of the Roman soldier anxiously performing his nightly sentry duty on Hadrian's Wall with the northern rains seeping through his protective armour, but it will not tell the historian what he is thinking nor, without an examination of the evidence, will it tell us much about the practice of sentry duties as the Roman army of occupation understood it. Similarly, re-enactment without imagination is likely to lead to a determination to play safe, an unwillingness to stray beyond what may be rethought by imagining, for example, what is responsible when a train of past thought is interrupted or when a sequence of past actions is incomplete.

Imagination in history is unlike imagination in art. Collingwood does not make history in any sense fictitious or unreal, since it is not the act of imagining which creates the unreality but what is imagined. But what is imagined may be accepted fact, as in my imagining Alcibiades in his cunning and frustration urging the

Sicilian Expedition on the cautious Athenians, or not fact at all, as in my imagining Adolf Hitler hard at work on his (later notorious) diaries. In other words, without the discipline of rules of inquiry and the availability of evidence, imagination in history is an unruly friend. But Collingwood does not consider that imagination in history is optional. The role he ascribes to it is 'not ornamental, but structural' (IH 241). Operating within history, the imagination is neither the gilding on the acquisition of fact nor the wholly capricious creation of possible worlds. But if imagination in history is neither decoration nor fancy, as Collingwood is surely right to insist, then what is it?

To common sense it must appear that one of the strengths of realism is its denial that historians know the past by imagining it. My imagining Plato obsessively designing new constitutions for Dionysus II of Syracuse does not make it true that he did. But whatever my authorities say about Plato's activities as a politician putting the philosophy of *The Republic* into practice they can never, as Collingwood points out repeatedly, be the final word. The primary role of the imagination, then, is to give historical method its cutting edge. By selecting the most plausible of his authorities, by filling in the gaps in the historical narrative – Caesar was in Rome on such and such a date and on the northern borders of the Empire at another – a gap which Collingwood tells us historians interpolate 'with a perfectly good conscience' (IH 240), and by criticizing – assessing testimony for trustworthiness, looking for inconsistencies in their sources and so on, historians aim to construct a narrative of the past which is coherent and continuous. Moreover, the exercise of the imagination itself discourages historians from making the twin errors of universalism and provincialism. Collingwood's new science of history refuses to draw inferences from human nature and it is more than just ordinarily aware of the dangers of assuming that the boundaries of the historian's world are also the boundaries of the historical world; hence his comment that the practice of infanticide in the ancient world 'is no less true for being unlike anything that happens in the experience of contributors to the *Cambridge Ancient History*' (IH 240).

Now if Collingwood's discussion of the historical imagination had stopped at this stage it might well be thought controversial, but hardly provocative. But it doesn't since Collingwood is determined to scatter realist pigeons further. Perhaps, Collingwood suggests, the historical imagination is able to tell us a lot more about history than realists and, possibly, even some non-realists allow. Perhaps the imagination tells us what history uniquely is. His first thought is that it is the historical imagination which enables the historian to go beyond fixed historical points. The imagination allows us to fill in the gaps in the historical calendar, so to speak, and to find links between the assured data in any specific web of belief. His second thought is much more radical. The historical reconstruction of the past is itself nothing other than the work of the historical imagination. For the historian there are no data on which to hang imaginative reappraisal. The assumption that historians work from fixed, stable and settled information, as from tablets set in stone, serves only to confine and distort history which leads Collingwood to the view that far from it being the case that it is past fact which controls the imagination it is actually the imagination which controls what is to count as past fact. In other words, it is the a priori imagination that is the load-bearing concept in history. And here Collingwood's position moves from provocative to startling because he argues that not only is the a priori imagination central to the work of historical construction it is the basis of historical criticism as well.

Collingwood tells us quite specifically what he understands the a priori imagination to be. It presents to us 'objects of possible perception which are not actually perceived: the underside of this table, the inside of an unopened egg, the back side of the moon.' In these cases, Collingwood says, 'we cannot but imagine what cannot but be there' (IH 242). Why is the imagination exercised a priori in such cases? Collingwood's choice of words gives us a clue – 'we cannot but imagine', by which he means that the imagination is the essence of the matter. It has the force of necessity about it. We may be sure, therefore, that the a priori imagination is not a form of conjecture. A physicist may posit the existence of a particular entity to explain why matter behaves as it does. Without this entity no really persuasive explanation is possible. But the conjecture will remain a conjecture unless and until the entity is discovered and proved to be necessary in the way the theory requires. Similarly, a detective may ask himself if a certain alibi might be false. He imagines the facts of the case differently. But once again whether his conjecture turns out to be true or false, or remains a conjecture, neither true nor false, depends upon ascertained fact. But the a priori imagination differs from conjecture because no fact could count against it. It does not rely on inference from known fact and it is quite independent of empirical evidence. Moreover, since it is absent of any content the a priori imagination is totally unlike any particular imaginary picture of the past. It is, in other words, a formal condition of understanding. Historians cannot but agree about it. It is something which it makes no sense to doubt.

The a priori imagination provides, as Collingwood writes, 'objects of possible perception which are not actually perceived' (IH 242). So on standing opposite the Great Pyramid at Giza I see one side, possibly a section of another, but what I do not see I imagine. I do not surmise the existence of the sides I cannot see. The question of conjecture does not arise. A conjecture may turn out to be true or false, but there is no sense at all in which I am able to see one side of the pyramid and yet think of the remaining sides as matters of speculation or hypothesis. Now Collingwood considers the a priori imagination to be central to history so there must be an equivalent certainty concerning objects of possible understanding in the past. I am an historian writing a history of the Great Pyramid. The past does not stand for me as an object of perception does for its observer. The past is unlike the underside of Collingwood's table or the inside of his egg. It is, of course, also unlike the back side of the moon, even though it may now be seen via satellite. There is, therefore, no sense in which in understanding the past I imagine what I do not see because with the past there is nothing to see, no equivalent to the top of Collingwood's table or the outside of his egg. There is, however, a sense in which the past would remain opaque to me unless I possessed the capacity to imagine what I do not see. Collingwood, perhaps a little misleadingly, sometimes refers to this capacity as innate or, a little more fortunately, as a priori. But his point is surely plain. Without the capacity to imagine things as they once were, history would be impossible. So when I stand in front of the Great Pyramid, what I actually see and what it is possible for me to see come to me in different ways. And when I write a history of the Great Pyramid, it is the past that comes to me in different ways. The pyramid itself together with its attendant blocks of stone is the past in the form of present evidence, but what is not present is the past as past, the historical life of the Great Pyramid from its inception, and this comes to me neither as description because there is nothing to describe nor as conjecture because there is no room for doubt, but as an object of the a priori imagination.

An idealist account of the relation between thought and experience is here being adapted to history. No less than the present the past is knowable only through the concepts we use to talk about it. But whereas knowledge of the here and now depends on our capacity to imagine what cannot but be there as much as on our perceptions of what is there, our knowledge of the past is different, since in the absence of any such entity as an observed past, the capacity to imagine the past, 'we cannot but imagine what cannot but be there', as Collingwood puts it, must assume greater importance. This is the force of Collingwood's point that 'the web of imaginative construction' which is the historian's picture of the past is 'the touchstone by which we decide whether alleged facts are genuine' (IH 244). With this move the separation of Collingwood's philosophy of history from realism must surely be complete. As Collingwood affirms, 'the historian's picture of the past is thus in every detail an imaginary picture and its necessity is at every point the necessity of the a priori imagination' (IH 245).

Now if Collingwood's account of the a priori imagination as something hardwired into historical thinking had stopped there, his critics may have held their fire. However, Collingwood takes his argument a step further. Not only is the a priori imagination the mainspring of the historian's work, 'it supplies the means of historical criticism as well' (IH 245). But, the critics will now ask, how can the a priori imagination operate both as a condition of historical thinking and its method? We may allow that no historian can work without an imaginary picture of the past which he aims to understand. We may also allow that such a picture provides the historian's truth criteria. Evidence would then be admissible by reference to 'the web of imaginative construction' which gives the historian his operating matrix. But this process of evidence investigation and trial depends on there being some identifiable content which is being put to the test and this cannot be the a priori imagination. The a priori imagination is entirely devoid of content. It depicts no fact. It does not depend on inferences from facts or from facts in the form of evidence. Against Collingwood, we might describe the a priori imagination as providing the capacity for historical thinking, but as doing no work at all in the day-to-day business of historical thinking itself. In other words, it is hard to see how the a priori imagination can be both the condition of history and the driving force of historical criticism. It can be one but not the other, and certainly not both.

Pin-pointing the exact role of the a priori imagination in history is Collingwood's problem. In other words, he needs to separate the historical from the fictional world, but the line dividing them appears to have escaped him. It is not that history occupies the realm of past fact while fiction is purely imaginative. As Collingwood certainly wishes us to see, both take the form of constructed narratives in which life is described at the writer's command. Plausibility – that vicissitudes of plot should be believed without question – derives from the unique force of the writer's imagination. History, however, is different. As Collingwood states, 'the historian's picture is meant to be true' (IH 246), but true in what sense? The most obvious answer for Collingwood to give is true in the sense of following on from the evidence, but nothing would follow on from the evidence unless the historian had the capacity to imagine it as following. So, to take a famous example, both novelist and historian can imagine what it must have been like to be the Princes in the Tower, but whereas the historian's imagination must bend the knee to the evidence the novelist's need not.

At this point Collingwood's claim that the a priori imagination acts as the means of historical criticism must surely lose all power. We may grant that the a priori imagination – the capacity to imagine what cannot but be there – is the mark of history proper. However, this rules out only what we might refer to as history manqué, something which looks like history, but just isn't: say, a list of dates, or a chronology of events. What is allowed and even encouraged is the possibility that historians might imagine the past differently. No two historians will see the past in exactly the same way. To be sure, it would be hard to think of them as visualizing the past at all if no a priori imagination was present, but its presence is no guarantee that the courses taken by their imaginations will be the same. In other words, the a priori imagination – essential to history, as Collingwood understands it – co-exists perfectly happily with accounts of the past which differ widely. Thus, for example, where one historian sees conspiracy, dark deeds and dirty hands, another sees diplomacy, innocence and the patriotic determination to serve the public good. It is at this point that the need for a criterion of historical truth which is closer to the day-to-day workings of the historian's mind becomes quite transparent.

Collingwood's attempt to clarify the differences between history and fiction emerges from these difficulties. The a priori imagination does a lot more than simply permit interpolation between known facts. To see a ship on the horizon at point x and then at point y, but not its movement in between creates a gap for interpolation to fill, perfectly intelligibly, in Collingwood's own view. And, yet, as Collingwood insists, in history known facts are never known solely as facts, but, at least in part, as constructions of the historical imagination. Unlike the novelist, however, who is bound only by the standards of fictional sense, the historian is subject to the requirement to understand the past as it happened, not as it might be invented or made up. So how, then, does Collingwood think of historical knowledge as truth conveying? Collingwood's answer is, first, that the historian's picture of the past is determinate in space and time. Novels may be set in real surroundings – the Yorkshire countryside, a nineteenth-century London tenement, the First World War – and take place in real time, but there is no necessity for them to be. Moreover, even when they are it remains the novelist's imagination which is calling the tune. Second, history must be self-consistent. Whereas there are many novels, each one unique to itself, there is only one historical past and everything in it is subject to the same constraints, whether temporal or topographical. Third, and most important, the historian's picture of the past stands in a specific relation to evidence. Whereas we might ask whether the actions of a fictional character are believable or not it would be strange to ask what evidence we have for them. And so it is evidence which, in Collingwood's view, is the crucial feature of historical truth. What is true in history is what can be justified by an appeal to the evidence. Further, Collingwood often speaks of evidence as providing the content for the a priori imagination. Evidence, then, is our next port of call. How, exactly, does it furnish the historian with historical truths?

The problem of historical evidence

We normally think of evidence as giving grounds for belief. A proposition or a state of affairs is true if and only if there is sufficient evidence to support it. Propositions and states of affairs arise in the context of practices and practices are rule-governed activities. Thus, what makes evidence acceptable is determined by the rules of the practice in question. In other words, evidence is commonly appealed to, demanded or rejected as insufficient and none of these procedures would be possible without rules governing what may be reasonably said. What counts as evidence varies. A scientific practice will look to evidence derived from observation and experiment. Witness statements count as evidence in courts of law, but are inappropriate in scientific research. The cry 'that's good enough for me' may be wholly convincing in one context and not at all in another. Even so, while standards for the admissibility of evidence differ, discussions over what is to count as evidence are as much about the rules of evidence as the evidence itself. In other words, it is not the ash on the carpet or the speck of dust on the sleeve that is significant, but whether or not they may be admitted as evidence at all. What is true of the admissibility of evidence is also a feature of its gathering. Accumulation of facts will not give you the breakthrough unless it is animated and directed by thought: as Collingwood remarks, 'you can't collect your evidence before you begin thinking' (IH 281).

Evidence does not come ready-made. So when the detective believes that he has found evidence of foul play he has already approached the facts in a particular frame of mind, or, as Collingwood expresses it, in the light of a given set of questions. Even when someone is caught in the act evidence is not ready-made, but simply unnecessary. What is to count as evidence – the footprint outside the window or the broken gatepost – arises only in the context of a process of inquiry. Once again we see Collingwood's anti-realism hard at work. Facts do not just present themselves to the inquirer; they become evidence only in relation to the questions the inquirer wishes to ask.

With this in mind Collingwood's insistence that the historian's sources do not automatically establish themselves as evidence becomes more understandable. History as testimony leads directly to history as scissors and paste, the arranging and re-arranging of previous accounts. But, as Collingwood argues, it is not what the sources report that makes history, but the treatment the historian gives them. Thus, in principle, anything could function as historical evidence so long as it is the answer to a question. It is one of the basic tenets of Collingwood's view of history that the historian can say nothing beyond what the evidence permits. Equally, for Collingwood, the past as past, the past in its completeness when it was once a present in which individuals lived and breathed, had memories and hopes for the future, can be of no interest to the historian because it can never be recaptured in its entirety. Given this, we will readily see why his understanding of evidence is important. For the historian, evidence constitutes something resembling a final court of appeal. Nothing can be settled without it.

While Collingwood says that anything can in principle operate as evidence it remains the case that in terms of practical method it is the historian's purpose that is the driving force. Thus, Collingwood asserts that 'evidence means facts relevant to a question, pointing towards an answer' (IH 485). So, when Collingwood himself asks what Hadrian's Wall was for the facts regarding the Wall, 'a wall-top 7 or 8 feet broad, to which access was provided only by ladders every 500 yards and narrow stairways a mile apart, lacking artillery, lacking bastions, and, above all, garrisoned only with an average of 150 men to the running mile' (R.G. Collingwood and J. N. L. Myres (1936), *Roman Britain and the English Settlements*, Clarendon Press, Oxford, 132) appear in a new light. The answer now comes from the facts understood not as facts only, but as evidence for the answer to Collingwood's question. The Wall was never intended as a defensive barrier, but as an elevated sentry-walk to deter marauders and smugglers.

In a case like Hadrian's Wall Collingwood's close association of evidence with the logic of question and answer works very well. Difficulties, however, are not too far away. According to Collingwood's doctrine of the living past, the past is not wholly separate from the present but overlaps with it. Collingwood terms this overlap as 'incapsulation' (A 98), the encasing of past thought in present experience. The historian is justified in saying only what the evidence allows, but if all evidence is present evidence (the residue of past fact which is made relevant to the historian by his present questions), then surely what the historian discovers is not the past, but the present construction of it. This problem is not one, but two. Is history about not what really happened, but only what the historian is licensed by the evidence to say happened? Where there is no evidence the historian must make it clear that history has given way to conjecture. In other words, if there is no evidence for X then X must be regarded by the historian as something which cannot be ascertained. Now Collingwood certainly conceives the historian's task as building 'a picture of things as they really were and of events as they really happened' (IH 246). Nor can his stress on the role of the imagination in historical writing be said to undermine this. But, for Collingwood, what really happened cannot be established independently of the evidence. Thus it appears that the critic's objection holds. It is not the past as such that is the object of historical knowledge, but the past in the form of present evidence. Now Collingwood's best response to this is surely the one he actually gives. The critic is working with a false dichotomy. It is not that the historian either knows the past as such or he only knows it through his evidence. It is not a case of either/ or at all. The historian's evidence is evidence of something, and that something is the past. That the historian understands the past from a present standpoint does not prevent it from being the past which is understood, any more, Collingwood believes, than my perceiving an object B from *here* prevents object B from being *there* (IH 158).

If Collingwood escapes from the first sub-problem he still has to face the second. The historian may well know the past only through the medium of present evidence, but present evidence depends on interpretation which means that the past the historian knows is always the interpreted past, never the real one. Moreover, since interpretations differ and since the past in its original state can never be recovered no single interpretation can ever be relied on. Historical knowledge is no more than interpretation. On Collingwood's account there is nothing to check one interpretation except another one. The notion of historical truth becomes obsolete.

There is much in Collingwood's anti-realism to encourage this objection. Since facts as facts do not arise unless the historian pictures them as evidence and since evidence does not arise unless placed in the spotlight of interpretation, it is tempting to conclude that Collingwood's critics must be right. There is, however, much that Collingwood can say in reply. First, historical knowledge may not be more than interpretation, but it is not less than it either. From the claim that evidence is always interpreted evidence it does not follow that there are no rules of interpretation. In fact, Collingwood spends a great deal of time specifying what these are. The historian builds a case, and although the historian is no lawyer able to call witnesses for cross-examination, there are still rules of the interpretation of evidence to be followed. Second, even if evidence does not speak for itself it does not follow that in speaking for it the historian merely intuits what it has to say. It is certainly tempting for critics to take this line because it is the one suggested by Collingwood's doctrine that the historian in grasping what happened also knows why. But intuition has no major role to play in either case. Historians, like lawyers, sense on occasion that there is something about the evidence that is not quite right; both may have to trust their intuitions when the evidence is lacking, and even when it appears to be overwhelming, but intuition is not the front-line player here. Collingwood's doctrine that when the historian knows what happened he also knows why depends on the historian understanding the thought involved. Collingwood's point is that once the thought is re-enacted that is all that is required. More importantly, no thought can be re-enacted unless there is evidence for it and evidence is not evidence unless it is the answer to a question. So Collingwood writes that 'question and evidence in history are correlative. Anything is evidence which enables you to answer your question – the question you are asking now' (IH 281). Collingwood's aim is to free interpretation not from imagination, but certainly from guesswork. Historical knowledge on Collingwood's account is knowledge of the past through the interpretation of present evidence.

Collingwood's permissiveness about evidence – that anything can in principle count as evidence as long as it is the answer to the historian's question – has sometimes struck his critics as too permissive. Two objections take us to the heart of Collingwood's position. First, there can never be good evidence for what is scientifically impossible. On the face of it this seems only too obvious. No historian is likely to be confident of evidence which is self-contradictory or which is believable only if the law of gravity, say, is suspended. To adapt Aristotle, fire burns both here and in Persia, whatever the historical witness may allege to the contrary. However, what seems obvious as a description of historical practice is not at all obvious to Collingwood. History does not simply copy the methods of the natural sciences; it has its own assumptions and modes of procedure. So when Collingwood visualizes the modern historian silent in the face of ancient portents, oracles and soothsaying, he is not abdicating his anti-realist stance.

Similarly, in permitting the historian to ask whether an event could have happened as the evidence describes, Collingwood is merely widening the questioning process slightly to allow the historian to raise, say, the kinds of questions which a forensic scientist might wish to ask. In other words, it is not scientific but historical possibility which Collingwood seeks to elucidate. And this means that it is still the logic of question and answer which is the test of what is to count as evidence and not the rules of scientific method per se.

And, yet, realist critics of Collingwood will say that this lets him off lightly. By admitting that evidence of past events is open to question on scientific as well as historical grounds Collingwood has to acknowledge that realism is at least half right. There can be no place in history for evidence which science tells us is impossible. Stories about Shangri-la, garden sheds that just vanish, guns that fire of their own accord and cars that simply exceed the speed limit outside the driver's control all sound no more convincing to an enquiring historian than they will do to a jury listening to an optimistic barrister. Historical knowledge is dependent on evidence, and evidence is subject to scientific scrutiny. Here a great deal hinges on the nature of the charge that Collingwood's critics wish to bring against him. Is it that in history evidence should operate in the same way as it does in science? If this is the accusation, then, as we might expect, Collingwood's defence is robust. Historical and scientific knowledge are different and any room for the latter in deciding what is to count as evidence in the former is marginal. But Collingwood's critics may wish to bring a different charge. By allowing evidence to be tested by reference to the standards set by science Collingwood shows that irrational or groundless beliefs have no place in history. On the first charge Collingwood is not being scientific enough, on the second he is being too scientific. But the defence to the second charge is as robust as the defence to the first. Collingwood's critics have confused the historian's subject matter with the evidence available for it. Collingwood's position is that evidence is not self-authenticating, but nothing in this limits history. In fact, Collingwood makes a point of distinguishing his view of the historian's subject matter from Enlightenment assumptions about universal rationality. He writes that 'to think of any phase in history as altogether irrational is to look at it not as an historian but as a publicist, a polemical writer of tracts for the times' (IH 77). And he attacks those he calls 'obsessed logical

thinkers' (IH 492) for distorting history by asserting 'fantastic
distinctions between the savage and civilized minds' (IH 492).
Thus, it is perfectly possible to imagine Collingwood writing not
just a history of events which purport to be miracles, not just a
history of religious beliefs and practices which include a belief in
miracles, but, as long as it is based on the evidence, a history of
miracles themselves.

Collingwood understands human purpose to be a condition of
history. Without an understanding of actions as necessarily linked
to purposes the historian's task of reconstruction would be impossible. Critics will say, however, that purpose fails as a condition of
history because it is too restrictive as a specification of historical
evidence. A history organized on this principle must leave too
much out. Human beings are not monarchs of all they survey.
Purposes often go unfulfilled. Aims are left hanging for no apparent
reason. Means do not always lead smoothly and efficiently to the
achievement of ends. History tells stories of failure as often as
success. Collingwood's reply is that what is a condition of history
is a separate matter from what is to count as evidence. Moreover, it
is mandatory for the critical historian to probe claims regarding the
achievement of purposes, military victories and the like, to assess
whether they were real or pyrrhic (IH 237). Further, Collingwood
makes a point of saying that historical questions are as much
concerned to identify failures of purpose as successes (A 128). But
what, the critic might respond, if purposes fail (or succeed) through
luck? Luck is the element of contingency in history, the face of
nature in human affairs, that which takes the fulfilment of purpose
outside human explanation and so beyond history as Collingwood
understands it. Again, Collingwood's response is robust. As far
as evidence is concerned nothing is ruled out in advance. The
ironies of history on which Hegel placed so much emphasis may be
brought within the historian's compass. As long as the unintended
consequence, for instance, is the answer to the historian's question,
as long, in other words, as it can be made intelligible, it can be
included as part of an historical account. Similarly, the inadvertent
is admissible as long as there is evidence for it, as long, for instance,
as the historian can convincingly show how the inattentiveness
arose and what it lacked attention to. Even the arbitrary and the
confused can be included as long as they are the best answers
available to the historian's questions. Even pure luck in the form

of the totally unexpected can be given narrative content, the storm which comes out of a cloudless sky to wreck the boats which carried the cargo, etc. Finally, Collingwood does not fight shy of contingency itself. In his generally sympathetic remarks on the English historian J.B. Bury (IH 147–51), Collingwood argues that contingency is not, as positivistic philosophers of history claim, the gap in the explanation which can never be filled, but another name for individuality, and individuality 'appearing in history only now and then in the shape of the accidental or contingent, is just that out of which history is made' (IH 150).

The problem of historical inference

Historical thinking, as Collingwood portrays it, is neither memory nor guesswork. It is reasoning of a special kind. So when Collingwood tells us that the historian reconstructs the past inferentially on the basis of the evidence we can be sure that he is telling us something important. Without inference there would be no history. Inference is common to the methods of science and history and we know that on Collingwood's account history is autonomous, which means that historical inference must be special. Exactly how special we will soon discover. It is worth commenting that Collingwood clearly wished to write more about inference in history and it is apparent also that what he did write he was not always satisfied with. Given its importance inference is not always treated with the depth it deserves, but even so we have both in *The Idea of History* and outside it sufficient material to build up a picture of what Collingwood wanted to say.

The leading principle of history proper is that the past is understood inferentially on the basis of present evidence. This is how historical knowledge comes about. And, yet, we need to be crystal clear that while it is inference which drives the historian's understanding it cannot explain the idea of the past itself. The past as a concept is one that belongs to human thinking a priori, or, as Collingwood explains, it is axiomatic that 'every historical event is situated somewhere in past time' (IH 109). That there is a past, that it is ordered necessarily such that one event follows another and that it is construed as the expression of human intelligence are preconditions of historical inference, not the results of one. A past which is more than merely an aggregate of unrelated events is a necessary condition of historical thinking. The past itself is, then, something that we cannot sensibly doubt, but how it appears to us and in what form are the subjects of historical investigation.

Collingwood's claims for inference arise out of his criticism of history conceived along the lines of scissors and paste. If the historian is to have knowledge of the past beyond the boundaries set by his authorities then asking the right questions in the right order and drawing the right inferences from the answers become the twin pillars of the new historical method. Historical knowledge is not empirical. The facts of history are past facts. They can be discovered only by 'a process of inference according to rational principles' (IH 176); to think of historical facts as apprehended empirically is to make it impossible to think of them at all. But the historical inference, as Collingwood understands it, is neither deductive nor inductive. It is not deductive because inferring in history is not isolated from content. In deductive logic knowledge of the world does not come into it. Proof consists in what follows from the premises, whether or not the premises are true. Nor is inference in history inductive. It is not based on observation or perception and it does not infer the existence of laws or generalizations from known instances. Historical knowledge shares deductive logic's capacity to demonstrate the rational necessity involved in specific kinds of reasoning, but it also concerns events occurring in specific places and at specific times. For Collingwood, therefore, the historical inference must be both compulsive and substantive.

There is, therefore, much more to Collingwood's account of historical inference than the claim that historical knowledge is organized on a scientific basis. All sciences defend assertions of knowledge by showing the evidence on which they are based. Inference, Collingwood wants us to see, is the logical face of history. The historian argues back from the present to the past. Moreover, Collingwood is telling us that these arguments possess a common logical form. What the logician calls premises the historian calls evidence. So when historians infer that such and such must be the case they are drawing conclusions from premises known to be true. Inferential knowledge is indirect. A belief that checkmate follows in two moves is inferred from other beliefs, that the player who is facing defeat has just lost his queen, is unable to castle out of check and so is forced to move his pawn, and so on. Inferences enable us to move compellingly beyond what we know to be the case. So when Collingwood, writing as an historian of Hadrian's Wall, argues inferentially, he concludes that if his account of the Wall's purpose is true then there must have been a system of towers beyond the end of the Wall operating as sentry-posts, although there is no observable or traceable presence of them. As we know, excavation confirmed Collingwood's hypothesis. In other words, given the truth of Collingwood's view of the Wall's purpose, that it was a sentry-walk, not a defensive system, his deduction that in order to fulfil that function it must have extended beyond its current area was correct.

In both examples inferences are drawn from what is already known to be true. Both are projections which lead us forward either to what must happen or to what must have been the case – checkmate in two moves or the existence of towers operating as signal stations. By reasoning inferentially Collingwood has shown us something necessary about a specific historical object in a specific historical circumstance. He has therefore established that historical inference can be both compelling and substantive.

We should be clear that inference belongs to history in a way that it does not to aesthetics. Understanding each page in a novel (unless it is a very bad one) is not a matter of the reader having to reconstruct what its author means, as if the text is a collection of marks or inscriptions, each as puzzling and mysterious as the next. But this activity of reconstruction – the step-by-step testing of hypotheses – is exactly what the historian's job consists in. This is why Collingwood says that historians do not find evidence, but make it (as opposed, obviously, to making it up) through the questions they ask and the inferences the answers enable them to draw. Indeed, Collingwood often speaks of inference as embracing the character of the historical judgement itself, so when he speaks about the relation between the historian's evidence and the conclusions drawn from it he terms it an inferential relation. Thus, identifying evidence as evidence – the broken Roman vase, the medieval manuscript, the twentieth-century politician's diary – and asking what may be inferred from it once identification has taken place are not two separate processes as they would be if they were terms in a syllogism, but one. For Collingwood historical argument is not a matter of, first, empirically identifying the trace of the past as it is found in the present and then, second, inferring what it means. That would make the historian's processes of thought too much akin to deductions from bald facts. Both processes are processes of interpretation. However, not all interpretation involves or requires inference. In some cases, to interpret an object – say, a piece of Italian pottery – and to see it for what it is are the same. Here it is not a matter of moving inferentially beyond known facts. In other cases, where to interpret and to see the object for what it is are not the same, drawing inferences from known facts to new conclusions is the only way of filling the gap.

One of the recurrent themes of Collingwood's discussion on inference is that historical arguments are capable of proof: not, we may be sure, proofs of a definitional or axiomatic kind, or even proofs that we think of as inductive or deductive, but proofs nevertheless. Collingwood stresses the critical and selective activity of the historian; in other words, the sort of work which gives the historian independence from his authorities. This is an essential feature of the autonomy of history as Collingwood understands it, but it also has a specific function in cases where the historian encounters a conflict between authorities or where the historian's interrogation of his sources fails to elicit answers to the questions put. Collingwood gives two examples. Both reveal inference at work in cases where there are gaps in the narrative or in the explanation of the event. In the first example the historian finds that his authority is silent on precisely the information that he wants to discover. Collingwood takes the case of Caesar's narrative of his invasion of Britain. The sharp-eyed historian will ask what Caesar's purpose was in mounting the invasion, but he will soon discover that Caesar says nothing about this, by contrast with his account of his invasion of Germany in which he says that everything he intended to achieve he did achieve. As Collingwood remarks, the inference to be drawn from Caesar's silence is that his intentions in invading Britain were not fulfilled. Caesar triumphed over his British enemies. He gained their tribute and their submission, but not the permanent conquest that he was aiming for. The conclusion – that Caesar's purpose in invading Britain was permanent conquest – is not stated, but inferred. Nevertheless, it follows from the evidence as the historian has ordered it. Thus, Collingwood maintains that inferential knowledge plays a major role in the historian re-examining his evidence in the light of this idea. In the second example the historian discovers how his authority can be made

to yield information that it did not possess. Collingwood asks us
to imagine a car mechanic inferring from a driver's description
of the faults exactly what the problem is. Similarly, the historian
can infer from his authority's account what his authority did not
know. Inferential reasoning allows the historian to converse with
his authorities, to challenge and, on occasion, to go beyond them.

Nevertheless, Collingwood's elucidation of the role of inference
in historical understanding is not free of trouble, since he argues
that an historical inference can prove 'its point as conclusively as
a demonstration in mathematics' (IH 262). Mathematical statements – say, $7+7=14$ – are true quite independently of what
they are about – say, apples or coconuts – just as a deductive
inference is valid quite independently of whether its terms are
composed of men called Socrates or Ps and Qs. But historical
inference is not true independently of its content. A brief return to
Collingwood's own treatment of Hadrian's Wall enables us to see
this. Collingwood's argument about Hadrian's Wall can be stated
deductively. Thus, all Roman sentry-walks are marked by sentry-
posts/Hadrian's Wall is marked by sentry-posts/therefore Hadrian's
Wall is a sentry-walk. Except, of course, that Hadrian's Wall as
Collingwood first examined it was not marked by sentry-posts
beyond its end, and so it could have been the first Roman sentry-
walk that had sentry-posts along its entire length, but was not a
sentry-walk at all. In other words, understood in terms of strict
deductive logic Collingwood's inference leaves the question open.
Not entirely open, of course, because a large number of explanations can be discounted, but open enough to say only that on the
available evidence, while it is probable that the Wall is a sentry-
walk we cannot be sure; that is, until the discovery of the towers
operating as sentry-posts beyond the end of the Wall clinched the
argument. Restating Collingwood's process more conditionally
allows us to see the kind of certainty it contains. If Hadrian's Wall
is a sentry-walk it will be marked by sentry-posts, but there are no
sentry-posts where there should be. Inferential knowledge tells us
that they should be there, while empirical investigation in the form
of excavation and examination confirms that they are.

When Collingwood speaks about pure historical methodology
he means something like pure detection. In these types of inquiries
deduction is all. However, as we have seen, statements about the
past are neither strict logical inferences nor empirically verifiable

in a straightforward manner. They are inferential in the sense that they convey what the historian thinks is possible and, if possible, what is believed to be the most plausible among a number of competing hypotheses. However, no single hypothesis can ever be totally reliable, since without weighing the validity of alternative hypotheses the dangers of error in accepting one as correct solely because it is consistent with the evidence are quite apparent. Similarly, historians commonly draw inferences of a kind which the rules of logic strictly understood would not sanction. Arguing that because there is no evidence that an event took place it did not happen is, according to Collingwood, routine among historians, yet it is hardly good logical practice.

When Collingwood's criticisms of formal logic are taken into account his view that history and logic sometimes part company is less surprising. Plausibility and probability now look to be the historian's benchmarks. They determine the best explanations that history can give. Should we conclude, therefore, that Collingwood's attempt to model historical arguments on logical ones has run aground? While it remains true that not any content can be persuasively injected into historical inferences it must surely be the case that reasoning from evidence lacks logic's seal of certainty. When from the windows of 221B Baker Street Holmes and his brother, Mycroft, reason their way to a description of a total stranger as an old soldier, NCO, ex-Indian army, a widower with a family, they could be right in all their premises and, if the man turned out to be the criminal genius Moriarty in disguise, completely wrong in their conclusions.

Collingwood wishes us to see that evidence is only evidence if it answers the historian's questions. Answers are important because they raise the next question to ask in an orderly and systematic manner. Collingwood's logic of question and answer was developed as his alternative to propositional logic. It plays a major role, too, in historical reasoning. It is, therefore, Collingwood's logic of question and answer that should concern us next.

The logic of question and answer

No doctrine of Collingwood's is, perhaps, more often criticized than his new logic of question and answer. Question and answer is vital to Collingwood's conception of how historians go about their work, and yet, in Collingwood's hands, it is not exclusive to history. It is a necessary feature of all thinking which aspires to be scientific. Indeed, Collingwood sometimes presents modern logic as a conspiracy to silence the historical masters of his new logic – Socrates, Bacon and Descartes (IH 273) – in favour of knowledge understood as apprehension of, or propositions about, the facts. By contrast, for Collingwood, any thinking worth the name approaches a given problem – say, the refusal of my car engine to start, the location of a medieval bridge, the authenticity of an eighteenth-century literary text or the identity of a twentieth-century assassin – first, with the relevant questions in mind, second, with new, perhaps more precisely targeted questions once the answers to the original questions have emerged, and third, in the recognition that this question-and-answer process is also a procedure which is ordered so that the correct answer may finally be found.

What is true about thought in general is also true about historical thought in particular. The historian is not a passive chronicler of facts, but an interrogator determined to test his subject matter to get at the truth. One of Collingwood's main criticisms of history as chronicle is that it leaves the historian entirely dependent on his authorities and so limits (and sometimes prohibits) the questioning techniques which Collingwood takes to be the key features of historical method. Thus, Collingwood writes, 'history finds its proper method when the historian puts his authorities in the witness box' (IH 237).

Collingwood's readers may well feel that the logic of question and answer is simply a commonsense description of how problem-solving actually works. Take away Collingwood's aim of replacing propositional logic and it is surely not difficult to see human understanding in the way he suggests. Collingwood does not, however, make this move himself and his attack on scissors-and-paste history would lose much of its force if historical method was simply a blend of statements and questions about the past. For Collingwood, historical method does not consist of propositions about the past at all.

The logic of question and answer is made up of a number of theses applying, first, to thinking in general, and second, to historical thinking in particular. Starting from the idea that discovering the meaning of what someone said or did requires understanding the question in their mind when they said or did it (see IH 219 where we find 'If it is by historical thinking that we re-think and so re-discover the thought of Hammurabi or Solon, it is in the same way that we discover the thought of a friend who writes us a letter, or a stranger who crosses the street'). Collingwood develops the main components of his new logic. These may be formulated as follows:

- *Thesis one* – There is a correlative relation between the question and its appropriate answer. Detailed and particular answers match detailed and particular questions. Generalized answers match generalized questions and so on.

- *Thesis two* – Propositions cannot contradict one another unless they are answers to the same question.

- *Thesis three* – Truth is not the property of propositions considered in isolation, but of question-and-answer complexes.

Collingwood gives his own example (A 32) of the logic of question and answer in practice. In tackling the problem of my car failing to start the handbook, which consists of a number of abstract propositions, will not help me. I must myself ask the right questions in the right order. I address the general question 'why won't my car start?' by reducing it to a number of specific questions such as 'is number one plug working?', the answers to which allow me to eliminate step by step the causes of the trouble. In practice, then, the logic of question and answer is ordered logically, substantive and compelling – it leads to the correct solution or allows me to eliminate the incorrect solutions to the problem at hand. Unlike my car, however, the past is not a compliant and immediate object of my attention. The past no longer exists. The historian can ask questions of the past, therefore, only if in some sense it can be made present. In addition, as we have seen, it is made present in the form of evidence, those traces of the past remaining in the present on which historical reconstruction is based. Now we may be sure that the logic of question and answer in its general formulation (theses one to three above) will apply to historical thinking in particular. But since the past is of a different order from the present any questioning of it will require further specification. This leads to the following theses:

- *Thesis four* – An historical question must be one that the historian thinks is answerable. This means that for an historical question to arise it must be related to evidence.

- *Thesis five* – In historical thinking question and evidence are related correlatively. Collingwood writes that 'nothing is evidence except in relation to some definite question' (IH 281).

- *Thesis six* – Question, evidence and knowledge in history are related. Collingwood writes: 'the only knowledge that the historian claims is knowledge of the answer which the evidence in his possession gives to the question he is asking' (IH 487).

The twin sources for Collingwood's new logic are his dissatisfaction with propositional logic and his close and detailed experience of archaeological investigation. As with many of Collingwood's ideas in history as well as in aesthetics, theory and practice are intimately related. Even so the theory behind the logic of question and answer has never been short of critics. It has been argued, for example, that far from displacing propositional logic the logic of question and answer is actually dependent upon it. If all statements are answers to questions, how can we tell which question the statement answers without an independent grasp of what the statement means? In other words, conventional accounts of truth have an awkward habit of resurfacing. So, if it is the case, as Collingwood says it is, that truth is a property, not of propositions, but of question-and-answer complexes then it must also be possible for question-and-answer complexes to be false, but in what sense false? One obvious sense in which a question-and-answer complex might be false is that one of the answers it contains is incorrect and so the chain of questioning it supports leads to the wrong answer. Collingwood does not deny (nor could he) that new evidence can challenge old answers to old questions and lead to better answers and new questions. Nor could he deny that some answers are better because they not only explain the evidence which supports a given hypothesis, but also the evidence which runs against it. Systematic questioning is at the centre of the historian's business. Sifting true from false, or, in Collingwood's language, sifting questions which take the inquiry forward from those that do not, involves putting the evidence to the test. Historians reach their conclusions inferentially, connecting them with the evidence by means of hypothetical propositions. If Caesar's purpose in invading Britain was a raid or a temporary occupation, then we should expect such and such to be the case. If the evidence for this is lacking, then the hypothesis must be re-examined and further questions asked. Unlike science, history does not depend upon the existence of general laws, nor does it depend as mathematics does upon axioms held to be necessarily true. And yet historical inference, including as it must the logic of question and answer, enables the historian to reconstruct the plans, motives and intentions of historical agents in a rigorous manner. Certainty in history may be found, but only on the basis of the evidence and the questions that historians ask of it.

CHAPTER FOUR

Arguing with Collingwood (II)

Past, present and future

Nothing reveals realist assumptions better than its view of the past as open to explanation in the same way as the present. Collingwood is absolutely clear that the past is categorically different. More importantly, Collingwood is telling us that without grasping what makes the past different the nature of historical understanding must always remain obscure. The past is the historian's working material. It is also an object to be explained. What makes the past categorically different, therefore, takes us to the heart of history.

The past does not disclose itself to the historian as nature does to the scientist. In part, this is because the past no longer exists and so it is not there to be observed or experimented on. But much more significantly, the past stands in a specific temporal relation to the present, and Collingwood believes that it is important to say something about this relation and why it is relevant to history. No philosophy of history, in other words, can ignore the problem of time. Collingwood quickly dismisses metaphorical explanations. Time is not a stream or a clock or, even, a straight line. More dangerous to the emergence of a genuinely historical understanding is the human habit of expressing temporal relations as spatial ones, so that, as Collingwood remarks, 'we suppose that the past still exists and lies somewhere concealed behind us' (IH 364). Setting this supposition aside is essential if history is to get to work autonomously, but we should be aware of where this leads us. The past has no existence, but the present does. Collingwood takes an important step when he says: 'the present alone is actual: the past and the future are ideal and nothing but ideal' (IH 364).

The key feature of the past, therefore, is that it is an ideal state. Much of importance follows from this. When Collingwood says it is the present alone that is actual, he is, in effect, telling us that knowledge of the past without present history, including its structure, presuppositions and manner of writing, is impossible. All history begins from the present. Moreover, all evidence is present evidence, and since the past is not always cooperative in terms of the traces of itself that it leaves behind, the evidence that does remain requires interpretation and selection. History is knowledge of the past, but there would be no knowledge of the past at all if history was naked of assumption, end or purpose.

Now if past and future are ideal states and nothing but the present is actual, what, then, is history? History is neither wholly the past nor wholly the present. History is, as Collingwood states, 'the reconstruction of an ideal object in the interests of knowing the present' (IH 406). Past and present, ideal and actual, are not, therefore, completely separate from each other. This is precisely what Collingwood's doctrine of the living past teaches. As a chunk of time the past is of no interest either in itself or to the present. But as the medium of human activities that once took place in a present, the past gains, if not grandeur, significance and autonomy. The living past, as Collingwood puts it, (IH 406) is not a point, but a world.

How, then, does the living past relate to the past itself, that is, to the past as it was? Collingwood's answer is not difficult to see. Historical knowledge is the re-enactment of past thought. But re-enactment does not consist of simulating what once was; nor is it a matter of empathy alone, a charitable bringing back to life of a lost existence. Nor, most importantly, is it a matter of reproducing the past in its totality, since if the past has disobligingly left no trace of itself then it cannot be examined in the present, and if it cannot be examined it cannot become an object of historical inquiry. The doctrine of the living past cuts both ways. Thus, not any past fact among the totality of past facts is of historical interest. As

Collingwood remarks, 'the favourite wine of the maternal grand-father of the standard-bearer who jumped ashore from Caesar's ships on the coast of Kent' (IH 406) is an historical question only in the abstract. Past fact – say, a listing of dates or a family tree, has no significance independently of historical thought, and historical thought is, for Collingwood, the deliberate and systematic recon-struction of the past on the basis of present evidence.

The historical past, then, is neither the past in its entirety nor the past when it was once the present, when it was once subjective experience. History aims to reconstruct the past objectively on the basis of the evidence. And the past as reconstructed by the historian is different from the remembered past. Memory is subjective and immediate. History, by contrast, is objective and mediate. There are two vital arguments at work here. First, the historian's job is not to relive the past as it was subjectively experienced. The historical account in which the sun rises over Mount Olympus is not the sunrise as Pericles experienced it upon his return to Athens. Second, the historian's job is not to remember the past as it was subjectively experienced. The historical account of Pericles' memories of the sunrise deploys evidence which Pericles did not need and which it would make little sense to expect. Does memory, then, have no place in history? Diaries, personal records, interviews with people who were there at the time, who, for example, actually experienced the London Blitz or, as children, were sent into the countryside to escape the bombing, do have a place in history, but as evidence, and so to be tested as evidence. Collingwood's point remains. Memory as such is not history.

The historical past is also different from the ideal and the recollected past. It is separate from the practical past, too. 'True history,' Collingwood writes, 'must be absolutely passionless, absolutely devoid of all judgments of value, of whatever kind' (IH 402). Collingwood is right to suggest that many will find this hard to accept, since it should surely not matter to our condemnation of evil that it occurred in the past. But Collingwood is insistent. First, the past remains the past whatever practical attitude the historian takes towards it. The past (as opposed to past behaviour by a present individual) is over completely, done with, nothing can change what happened. The massacre at Corcyra (Collingwood's example, IH 404), or the atrocities at My Lai during the Vietnam War (my example), are over, nothing can alter them. Second, practical attitudes are designed to make a difference. The whole point of the practical attitude is to bring about a change in the world. So it would be odd, or at least would require explanation, if I condemned, say, the death penalty and yet did nothing to help end it when the opportunity arose. But in the case of the past no opportunity can arise. The practical past (what Collingwood sometimes calls the pragmatic past) is empty here. If there is an appropriate practical response to the past it is, Collingwood suggests, sadness; he writes: 'we need only recognize clearly that these things have been; they are over; there is nothing to be done about them; the dead must be left to bury their dead and to praise their virtues and lament their loss' (IH 404).

Collingwood's separation of the practical from the historical past is contentious, since even though he hopes (almost certainly vainly) to prevent history from becoming a moralist's stamping ground objectors point out that his methods of doing so are shaky. The idea that past events, including acts of great humanity as well as immense brutality, are unalterable is little more than a truism, a definition of the past. The point in praising past virtues and condemning past vices is that they should not be forgotten. It is not necessary to adopt a legalistic model of responsibility to achieve this. Striking an attitude towards the past is no different from striking an attitude towards the present. Thus, apologizing for the crimes of earlier generations need not be insincere so long as efforts are made to prevent their reccurrence and that the present generation understands the apology for what it is.

Critics will argue further that the idea of a living past is a licence for moral judgements in history, since it suggests that the separation of present from past is never total. While 'the actual, the present, is the only possible object of our knowledge, field for our activity, and stimulus to our feelings' (IH 404), the present, for Collingwood, is never wholly the present, but contains traces of a past which in being known historically enable us to understand how the present has come to be what it is. This falls well short of a justification for liberal Anglicanism, but it does point to the possibility of learning from history and this in turn rests on the belief that the past is not wholly past but contains lessons for the future.

Collingwood's sense of the present as the immediate and ongoing gives it priority over past and future which are ideal states, but past and future are not ideal states of the same kind. Both are abstractions, but whereas the past no longer exists, the future has yet to exist. It is tempting, therefore, to think of the past as that which is wholly unalterable and the future as wholly alterable, open to every possibility, a function of human choice and volition. The future is an open book. We can write in it what we will. The problem with this is that it makes the future look too much like the past. The past is unalterable because what has happened cannot be undone, but what cannot be undone is known historically only from the standpoint of the present, and this means that it cannot be known directly. But this is the case with the future, too. If the future is the realm of the possible then it can be known only by hypothesis, so, for example, if we carry on consuming energy at the current rate, in 50 years' time disaster will strike. The present alone is actual, Collingwood tells us, but he clearly cannot be content with a conclusion that puts historical knowledge on the same level as astronomy.

There is one solution to this problem which Collingwood rejects out of hand. He rejects the idea put forward by Spengler and others (see IH 181–2, 220) that relations between past, present and future are cyclical. In a contemptuous aside Collingwood dismisses those who search the past for trends, uniformities and recurrences: 'in order to pigeon-hole historical facts, the living body of history must first be killed (that is, its essential character as process must be denied) so that it may be dissected' (IH 163–4). The historian is no prophet. The claim that history can foretell what will happen on the basis of what has happened is the complete opposite of history. It is, as Collingwood comments, 'the conclusive mark of non-historical thought' (IH 182). There is no doubt that you do not solve Collingwood's problem by ignoring it. What you can do is approach the problem as Collingwood himself does. The future is the realm of the possible. We think of it in hope or apprehension, possibly fear. The past, by contrast, has the force of necessity. We think of it with regret or satisfaction, possibly pride. Hoping that something will turn out well is not the same as betting or guessing that it will, but like, bets and guesses, hopes also fail or go wrong. Regrets and satisfactions are different. It would make no sense to speak of regretting what did not take place or being satisfied by what you did not achieve. The disquieting solicitor's letter would not be disquieting unless it was a matter of history that the threats it contains are true. Statements about the past, then, are not hypotheses, but open to corroboration as far as the evidence allows. The past, in Collingwood's words, 'in spite of its unreality, can be the object of critical and rigorous inferential thinking' (IH 413). Or, as Collingwood writes in *The Principles of History*, 'all historical evidence is a medium through which past events have an impact on the mind of the historian; medieval charters no less than solicitors' letters' (PH 113).

None of this should be taken as saying that the course of history is determined by God or progress or freedom. While Collingwood insists that knowledge in history must be expressed in narrative form his point is not that there is some pre-existing pattern to events, but rather that the ways human plans and intentions work themselves out cannot be grasped as a Nautical Almanac is grasped. There is, however, one feature of human plans and intentions which Collingwood says historians cannot know. Historians re-enact the thoughts which ground human intentions, but the feelings which accompany them, the hopes and fears which often rouse them, must be permanently off-limits. Emotions are closed to re-enactment, and, hence, to history. It is to this alarming claim that we will now turn.

The limits of history: thoughts and feelings

Collingwood is famous for his assertion that past emotions are beyond the historian's reach. On first sight this seems a curious position to take up. Drop the feelings evident in past human activities and history becomes little more than an intellectual puzzle. The reasons (and possibly even the causes) behind the revolution are discoverable, but the elation of the successful revolutionaries (or the courage of the unsuccessful ones when they are about to be shot) is not. Surely, Collingwood's critics will say, history written on these terms must be a bloodless affair, aloof from gut feeling and instinct. Since it is often gut feeling that drives human beings forward, particularly at times of crisis when reasoning is often an imperfect guide, any history which leaves the emotions out will not be true to what it is about. As this is a conclusion that Collingwood surely does not want, his position is in need of explanation, but first we must be clear that this is his position and establish why he believes that it should be held.

Collingwood's exclusion of human feelings from history brings together (not always satisfactorily) arguments in philosophical psychology and the philosophy of history, but it is also less radical than it appears. What Collingwood says is that history proceeds by the re-enactment of past thought on the basis of present evidence. What is not thought – perception, instinct, feeling, appetite, desire, emotion – is not history. Thus, what Napoleon's feelings meant to him as he experienced them is firmly closed. But it is hard to imagine Napoleon's feelings meaning anything to him unless he was, first, conscious of them and, second, had given thought to them in some way. He may, for example, have tried to pin down what he was feeling, asked himself whether he was right to feel as he did, and whether he could change or overcome what he felt. Thus Napoleon's feelings can be known insofar as the historian can discover evidence for what he thought about them. Further, since Napoleon did not spend his exile in isolation, the thought of his companions about his feelings can also be known. Collingwood's exclusion clause now narrows. As long as past feelings are connected with past thoughts, they are open to historical knowledge. Past feelings that are unrelated to thought are shut off from re-enactment.

Why should we assume, however, that re-enacting the thought enables the historian to revive the feeling? Napoleon's companions did not require evidence in order to know what he was feeling. They could see his restlessness and frustration. By contrast, historical experience is necessarily indirect or second-hand. History, as Collingwood puts it, 'is not immediate self-enjoyment, it is reflection, mediation, thought' (IH 188). It is not, in other words, the past feelings themselves which are closed to history, but their immediacy. But in their immediacy neither thought nor feeling is open to re-enactment, so what makes feeling different? The answer is that feeling is nothing more than the immediate experience of it and so Collingwood concludes that past feelings cannot be historically known.

We find Collingwood's rejection of mind/body dualism both inside and outside *The Idea of History*. Feelings are not private inner states knowable only by introspection. We learn to express feelings in language and we share a common response to particular emotional experiences. There is an intellectual component to our emotional life which distinguishes it from pure sensation. And yet, for Collingwood, all emotion is felt emotion. The presence of subjectivity is ineradicable. 'Thoughts,' Collingwood writes, 'can corroborate or contradict each other, but feelings cannot' (PA 159). Here is the most significant clue so far to Collingwood's refusal to grant past feelings the badge of re-enactment. Human feelings are mortal. They die with us; once past they can never be made present. And Collingwood's reason for saying this should now be clear. Without the tears in my eyes (and it is important that they are mine) my feelings of sadness at the death of a friend would be merely the report of a neutral observer on an independently bodily state. I may reflect on my grief and others may testify to what I am feeling, but the historical re-enactment of my reflection does not produce the grief, and, as we have seen, for Collingwood, testimony is third-party evidence and, necessary though this often is, it is not history.

One argument against Collingwood here is that his under-standing of human feelings is too narrow. Unlike purely physical sensations such as an ache or a sneeze, feelings are related to objects. I cannot literally feel anger at anything. I cannot feel pride about anything whatever. It must be something that I have done and it must be an achievement of some sort. Moreover, our behaviour is often a poor indicator of what we feel. Thus, for example, whether my waving my arms about reveals genuine fear or a phobia is not always discoverable by my actions alone. Further, what we feel does not necessarily follow from our descriptions of events. X and Y can both see that they have been subject to a practical joke, but whereas X thinks the situation hugely funny Y takes offence. In order to refine our understanding of what is going on in cases like these we need to expand the context a little by exploring what objects can be felt about intelligibly and why. Collingwood's opponent will now press his criticism home. This understanding – of object and of context – is surely historical in character. That we are talking about past or present feelings makes no difference. Feelings are related to objects and to contexts, and since these are necessarily imbued with ideas they can be re-enacted and so they can be made subjects of historical enquiry, as long as there is evidence for them.

Collingwood's response to this is not difficult to reconstruct. Raising the cognitive status of the emotions is not in itself the objection. In fact, there are many passages in Collingwood's writings where he makes precisely this move himself. But re-enacting a past feeling is different. Past feelings can be simulated, possibly even enhanced, as they are by actors playing historical roles. Past feelings can be sympathized with, possibly even made common cause with, as they are with past victims of discrimination, say, or exploitation. But re-enactment is not simulation and while empathy may add to its effectiveness, re-enacting past thought can proceed without it. Historical re-enactment is not an echo of a past event, nor does it merely repeat it, as one hiccup follows another. What is re-enacted is past thought, something better described, perhaps, as a process of reasoning leading to decision or action; in other words, a process, either theoretical or practical, which can be reconstructed in the thinking of the historian. Now we know two things about thought that are highly relevant to this point. First, as Collingwood understands it, thought is not only immediate, restricted only to one context of performance or discussion. An argument by Plato in the fifth century or by Descartes in the seventeenth century 'because it is a thought and not a mere feeling or sensation', as Collingwood puts it (IH 301), can exist both in its original context and in the historian's reconstruction of it. By following the stages of thought the historian does not produce an argument which resembles Plato's. Insofar as the argument has been understood correctly it is Plato's. Second, re-enactment is not a purely descriptive or neutral exercise. It is critical in the sense that the historian tests the re-enacted thought process and the conclusions it leads to. Thought, Collingwood tells us, is open to corroboration, and in re-enactment this is achieved by the historian examining alternatives, investigating possible inconsistencies and contradictions, identifying special pleading and so on. All of this works very well with strategies, arguments and plans of action which are open to assessment in terms of their rationality or reasonableness. It also works well with the re-enactment of purposes. But although feelings have objects which can in some cases be described as purposes, it is not by reference to their objects that we understand them. Napoleon did not reason his way to his feelings during his exile. Alexander did not reason his way to his pride in the Greek Empire, even though he made an empire to be proud of, one, moreover, whose aims and purposes the historian can reconstruct. Thus, feelings have no place in re-enactment. As

Collingwood says, 'the scent of the flowers and the breeze in his hair' (IH 295) can be remembered, but memory is not history. In the memory past and present are unavoidably tangled together. Absent the evidence which is the historian's guide in the memory nothing is impartial, nothing objective.

Collingwood's commentators may still think that he has taken a step too far. What objection is there to thinking of historical knowledge as in part re-enactment and in part imagination? After all they will point out, rightly, that Collingwood, in regarding the re-enactment of past thought as 'an integral element' (IH 290) in history, is in fact suggesting that there are other elements that may be relevant, but not integral. Thus, in order to understand a politician's strategies the historian must re-enact them. The fits of rage at his subordinates when they fail to carry them out cannot be re-enacted, but they can be imagined. Moreover, they can be imagined as a result of the historian asking the appropriate question – what would it have been like to have received a dressing down like that? As long as there is sufficient evidence the historical imagination can tell the historian what it must have been like.

Broadening the subject matter of history beyond the intellectual is a development in Collingwood's view of history that many of his critics welcome. In *The Principles of History* (in ch. 2 written in 1939, some three years after the passages in *The Idea of History* which deal with the emotions), Collingwood seems to do exactly that, except he doesn't. It is therefore important to see why he doesn't. Collingwood takes the case of an historian wishing to explain the construction of a fort in Roman occupied Britain. In addition to the requirements standard to Collingwood's conception of historical method – the discovery of evidence, the interpretation of it to establish intention and purpose, the gaining of insight into the mind of the officer who commands the fort to be built – the historian must also grasp the emotions which accompany the thought. Collingwood calls these 'essential' (PH 68) emotions. They are emotions without which the thought would not be what it is. Thus in the case in point the thought and the emotion match each other. The thought that the fort must be built to provide protection against danger rests on the emotion that fear is what danger induces. Here is an example of a past emotion that is historically relevant. Whatever other emotions the officer felt may be biographically relevant, but it is only the emotion which attends the thought that counts for the historian.

And, yet, it is open to doubt whether this argument gives the emotions the passport to history that Collingwood wants because in choosing this particular example he is surely privileging his own case. Fear as rational prudence involves thought in the form of an estimate of the risks of attack and the degree of protection needed, but fear as a basic instinct does not. A Coriolanus figure may well order the fort to be built for reasons of strategic necessity, but certainly not out of personal fear of the enemy. And personal emotions do count in history. In some cases the thought can be construed independently of the emotion where, as Collingwood puts it, the emotion is relevant only biographically. And in others, as in Collingwood's fort commander example, the emotion is the appropriate accompaniment to the thought. To establish whether or not fear is an intelligible emotion it is necessary to examine the context – is the threat real? Is the commander being over-cautious, as might be the case when the enemy had suffered a massive defeat and there were no forces capable of mounting an assault? Is the commander routinely fearful? Or is he not at all fearful, but capable of prudential action nevertheless? Teasing out the relationships involved is the true business of history as Collingwood understands it. But this opens the door only to emotions connected with thought. In cases where the emotion acts alone or where the emotion overwhelms the thought it is the emotion that is the spur to action. Achilles cannot think of Patroclus without longing for him, and it is the longing which determines what Achilles does.

Collingwood's broadening of its subject matter is, then, hardly a resounding endorsement of the emotions in history. This comes about because Collingwood too readily links the emotions with thought or rational purpose. What concerns the historian is the fort's purpose and the effectiveness of the engineering methods employed to construct it. Anything that is irrelevant to this concern whether to do with thought or the emotions – and relevance here is established by evidence – is transferred from history to biography. Collingwood's sharp distinction between history and biography is hard at work here, as it is in *The Idea of History* itself. It is a distinction that many have considered too sharp, and so we should spend some time looking at it further.

Past lives

Collingwood is not simply critical of biography; he is scathing about it. And, yet, the past would be unrecognizable if it was studied purely in terms of abstract categories. The past is what was once present and what was once present were individuals who saw themselves as individuals, not as merchants, slaves, kings and queens, peasants or, even, citizens, and almost certainly not as statistics. Whether it is the English Civil War or the life of Charles I the historical object is the individual. Thus, for Collingwood, the historian's object of study is determinate – 'what the historian thinks about is Elizabeth or Marlborough, the Peloponnesian War or the policy of Ferdinand and Isabella' (IH 233). But when the historian's object of study is the life of a single individual – Elizabeth I, say, or Lenin – how can historical investigation proceed except biographically? But, for Collingwood, biography is, apart from the motives of 'cattishness' (PA 87) and 'gossip-value' (PH 70) which he imputes to its practitioners, neither art nor history. As pseudo-art biography is amusement. As pseudo-history biography is scissors and paste, the gluing together of episodes from a life in order to excite, distract or entertain.

Here we need to retrace our steps a little. For Collingwood all history is the history of thought. In order to understand, say, Caesar's action in crossing the Rubicon the historian must re-enact the thought in Caesar's mind, and this means 'apprehending the individuality of a thing by thinking oneself into it, making its life one's own' (IH 199). We may well believe that this is exactly what biography at its best aims to do – to understand a human life on its own terms. But for Collingwood history requires something more. The historian in re-enacting Caesar's thought must also determine its significance as an assertion of state power or a method for disposing of one's political enemies, or both. Caesar in the historian's hands is an historical, not a biographical individual. Thus Collingwood writes: 'individual acts and persons appear in history not in virtue of their individuality as such, but because that individuality is the vehicle of a thought which, because it was actually theirs, is potentially everyone's' (IH 303). In re-enacting Caesar's thoughts the historian aims for an explanation which moves beyond what is local and temporary. Biographical facts, namely that Caesar's actions were performed by a particular individual at a particular time in particular circumstances, remain relevant, but their relevance to the historian is not the same as their relevance to the biographer. So when, in *The Principles of History*, he says that 'the history of a thought has nothing to do with the names of the people who think it' (PH 75), Collingwood is not denying that biographical information is relevant to history. Without a name the biographer has no subject, but that point may apply to historians, too. Equally, anonymity, in the shape of ignorance of names and dates of birth and death, is not in itself an obstacle to historical knowledge (PH 75). He makes a related point when he states that indexes and bibliographies of sources, while being useful to the historian, are worlds away from true historical research, something which starts when the historian makes the evidence his own.

Even so, Collingwood does say firmly that biography 'is not only non-historical but anti-historical' (IH 304), 'however much history it contains' (IH 304). How can this be? How can a biography not be history if it is already history? How can a biography which is already substantially historical be opposed to history? The answer is found in Collingwood's aspect theory (PA 43). Consider what Collingwood says about the difference between art and craft. Art is not a means to anything beyond itself; craft, by contrast, is precisely that. But this does not mean that the same object – say, an ancient Greek vase – cannot be in one aspect art and, in another, craft. What is important is that these aspects are not confused. Thus a work of art can also be useful or uplifting, but it is not because it is either or both that it is considered art. A building may be primarily an artefact, something constructed for a specific purpose, and it may also be art, 'but what makes it a work of art is different from what makes it an artifact. A representation may be a work of art; but what makes it a representation is one thing, what makes it a work of art is another' (PA 43).

When looked at in this light Collingwood's distinction between biography and history becomes more understandable. Collingwood distinguishes sharply between human life considered as natural process and human life considered as action. Thus, an individual life is in one aspect a structure of biological events containing 'all the accidents of animal existence' (IH 304), and in another, action, self-consciousness or thought. Within each single life, as Collingwood puts it, 'the tides of thought, his own and others', flow crosswise, regardless of its structure, like sea-water through a stranded wreck' (IH 304). Individuals can be both biographical and historical subjects, but the limits set by biography are not those set by history. All will be well, therefore, as long as these limits are not confused. History's limits are established by thought. What is not thought is closed to re-enactment. Biography's limits are established by natural process. Thus, a biography must include events in its subject's life some of which do not embody thought – sensations, desires, feelings – together with the 'the accidents of animal existence' referred to earlier, some of which do embody thought, but are included because they may entertain, instruct or divert the reader. And, yet, Collingwood has acknowledged that as the story of an individual's life is more than just a medical bulletin or a gossip column, it must also contain much that is genuinely historical. But this, finally, is Collingwood's point. Just as a heavily representative painting may still be art so also a biography substantially weighted with its subject's biological exigencies may still be history. To paraphrase Collingwood, a biography may be a work of history, but what makes it a biography is one thing, what makes it a work of history another.

Critics of Collingwood will have more than a word to say at this point. They will say that Collingwood has wrongly run together two distinctions – one between natural and human process, the other between biography and history. Collingwood may well be right to say that there can be no history of nature, but this surely applies to biography, too. What gives biography its structure – what determines its particular aspect, if you like – are not natural facts, but the individual's perspective on their life understood as a whole. The skilled biographer not only relives the life of his subject, he enhances it through the telling. In the biographer's hands, events in life which his subject made too little of or repressed can be induced to say more. Such filling in the gaps is a significant part of the history, too, but there is a difference. When the historian rethinks past thought the thought is not relived as 'a mere echo of an old activity' (IH 293), but is critically re-enacted as thought. In other words, in history it is not thought as a mental occurrence that is revived, as it is in biography, but thought as argument, something that is not only capable of being repeated, but also criticized and extended. Biography moves under the shadow of mortality whereas thought, Collingwood may be taken as saying, does not.

Collingwood wishes us to see that history is systematic knowledge. Its purpose is not to provide emotional satisfaction, but 'to command assent' (PH 73). Everything that makes history systematic points towards it being a body of knowledge that is publicly assessable, open to corroboration by others following through the same stages of questioning as the historian followed. Thus, re-enactment is in principle not only the method by which historians understand the past; it is also the method by which historians examine and test present inferences. In Collingwood's justly famous image (IH 266), the historian is a detective whose investigations can be reconstructed in order to detect false steps in the argument or conclusions for which there is little or no evidence. And, yet, in Collingwood's view, the historian is no reasoning machine. What makes history possible is that the past is present in the form of evidence and that the historian is receptive to it. But, even when evidence is available Collingwood recognizes that the historian may lack sympathy for what it reveals. When historians are antipathetic to their subject matter the result Collingwood says is not history, but dryness. A thought, a decision, a policy or a way of life into which the historian is unable to enter can be explained as fact, but not as history (IH 305).

What is a professional hazard for historians must also surely be one for biographers, too. A religious life written by a biographer who is unsympathetic to faith or to the idea of a life spent in the service of God is likely to remain dead on the page. Sameness of view, however, can be just as fatal. But whereas attentiveness and imagination (together with the discipline of the writer) enable biographers to overcome their own feelings the historian requires something more. To bring the past alive something more than sympathy is required. Thus, Collingwood argues that when we enter sympathetically into the immediate experience of others, imagine and possibly feel what they are feeling, we are not re-enacting their feelings, 'we are merely contemplating them as objects external to our present selves, aided perhaps by the presence in ourselves of other experiences like them' (IH 302–3). Thus when we encounter a modern biographer arguing that biography supports historical understanding 'by attending to the tone of voice' of the subject and by 'accumulating personal facts that will allow us to see what is said in a different light' (see Ray Monk (2001), 'Philosophical Biography: The Very Idea', in James C. Klagge (ed.), *Wittgenstein,*

Biography and Philosophy, Cambridge: Cambridge University Press, 4) we notice how far removed this is from Collingwood's position. For Collingwood nothing can become history except the thought itself, and even then not the thought in its immediacy, but the thought as the historian re-enacts it. There is, then, no tone of voice and no personal facts independent of thought. Collingwood's antidote to the historian's lack of receptivity is unfortunately vague. He talks of the historian needing to write from 'the organic unity of his total experience' (IH 305). No doubt historians and biographers can intrude their personalities into the stories they tell. Thus we may conclude that allowing the past life to speak for itself is as much an imperative for the historian as it is for the biographer. But Collingwood reminds us forcefully that their activities should not be confused. What, then, of autobiography? If biography is fundamentally anti-historical because its limits are those of natural process then surely autobiography must be, too.

In fact, Collingwood not only allows that autobiography is historical; he encourages his readers to think of it as such. Autobiography is 'a strictly historical account of my own past' (IH 295). Collingwood advises that the first task of the autobiographer is recollection which involves the discovery and identification of past experience. Searching the memory, however, delivers only the past as spectacle. What the autobiographer sees is himself as he was, but seeing himself as he was is not by itself history. For autobiography to become history it must also take on a second task which is to recount its subjects' thoughts. Recollection, even the recollection of thought, must always face the danger that the autobiographer will read back into the past ideas which did not come to him until later. Thus, autobiography can be history in the proper sense only if the writer can re-enact his past on the basis of the evidence.

Autobiographies are written for personal reasons, but Collingwood's point is surely that they can be truthful only if they are written historically, and that can happen only if they are connected with thought and based on evidence. Autobiography is, however, a curious genre. Since each piece of autobiographical writing belongs to a present standpoint the past is never brought home to the reader solely on its own terms. Rather the past is conspired with in order to express the first-person perspective on life that the author has reached. The biographer has the evidence of the whole life in front of him. The autobiographer is complicit in the story he wishes to tell. In the Preface to his own autobiography Collingwood famously wrote that 'the autobiography of a man whose business is thinking should be the story of his thought'. It is a comment we should consider further.

If autobiography is to be history, then it must be the history of its author's thought, but, in Collingwood's case, we might ask why? Is it because all history is the history of thought? Or is it because as a philosopher Collingwood deems nothing relevant to the particular story he wishes to tell other than his thought? Collingwood argues that all history is the history of thought because only thought can be re-enacted. Sensations, desires, feelings and emotions are, in their immediacy, closed to re-enactment. So the autobiography of a man of feeling – say, the *Memoirs of Casanova* – may be considered as history only if Casanova presents his desires as thoughts, since he may be showing the reader what it was like to live his kind of life. But Casanova's kind of life was not the life that Casanova lived. Casanova's life in its immediacy is not a kind of life at all, but life as Casanova lived it. Something of the character of a life lived wholly at the dictate of desire can be conveyed in letters and diaries, but even in these the original urgencies of assignation and embrace are impossible to recapture. Surely, then, what Casanova's *Memoirs* reveal is his past life understood from the perspective of his present reflection on it. Since past desires cannot be re-enacted the autobiography of a man of feeling can be historically enhanced only by its author connecting his desires with his thought, but his desires connected with his thought are not his desires as he first experienced them.

The autobiography of 'a man whose business is thinking' faces a different paradox. Casanova's problem is that of expressing what cannot be re-expressed. Collingwood is telling the story of his thought, but while thought makes history possible it does not determine the nature of the telling or what is told. Thus, the autobiography of an engineer, say, would be history only if it was the story of his past thought, but what story is told and within what limits is a matter of autobiographical choice. Collingwood in writing his autobiography chose to make it the story of his philosophical and historical thought. Unlike other philosophical autobiographies Collingwood's rarely strays beyond the brief he sets himself. The veil over his personal life is hardly ever lifted which means that his autobiography is history in the strict sense that Collingwood imposes. His past philosophical thoughts about the nature of history are re-enacted, the kinds of problems he faced are re-created and his solutions to them rehearsed with his present views clearly put on display. In other words, under-standing arguments in philosophy is inseparable from evaluating them. The 'tone of voice' together with the 'personal facts' that Ray Monk considers make all the difference simply do not reach the autobiographer's agenda, as Collingwood interprets it. In his autobiography Collingwood does not re-write his past thought, but he does present it in the light of his present concerns. Indeed, for Collingwood, if the autobiographer is also to be the historian of his past then he can do no other because history is not only the history of thought; it is present history as well.

Collingwood took the view that what the autobiographer could achieve by way of reconstructing his own past the historian could also do for others. Within the limits set by the re-enactment doctrine and on the basis of the evidence, history may properly be said to be a form of knowledge. Thus, Collingwood writes that of past individuals, 'we can know, so far as there is any knowledge, that the thoughts we create were theirs. (IH 296). In other words, there is a difference between the fictional past – say, the past of the historical film or novel – and the historical past. If there is a difference it is clearly one that we need to explore further.

Facts and fictions

Collingwood thinks of historical knowledge as autonomous. It is a body of knowledge arranged systematically, employing its own distinctive methods and procedures. The historical past is different from the scientific past. A given past event – say, the Russian Revolution of 1917 – may be understood as an instance of a general law explaining the incidence of revolution. But this, we may be sure, is not history as Collingwood understands it. Art, too, has wished to make the past its own. Unlike science, the achievement of art is to see a past event not as an object to be explained, but as the focus of the artist's imagination. In art proper, therefore, nothing constrains artistic effort except the emotions the artist is concerned to express together with his capacity to express them. Where the past is the medium of the artist's purpose, however, we encounter not art proper, but craft. Here the past is used as a means to produce a specific effect – the arousing of patriotic feelings, say, or the 'futile nostalgia for the past' (IH 87) that Collingwood associates with Romanticism.

It is part of the historian's job to dispel pictures of the past that are arbitrary or fanciful. Art and history each understand the past on their own terms. Hybrids, like the historical novel, may be compelling as craft, but they must remain false as history and, of course, as craft they are not art. And, yet, we should not misunderstand Collingwood here. Art and history are resistant to amalgamation, but not to resemblance. Imagination is hard at work in both. Moreover, imagination is not essentially unguided or capricious. What is imagined may be the world of past fact which the historian is trying to enter and explain, or it may be the fictional world that the novelist wishes to construct. We can grant that facts in history are never naked of interpretation and inference, but this serves only to reinforce the complex processes of investigation which make up the historian's world. We can grant, too, that the novel often contains much by way of factual reference, that the lives of fictional characters are often portrayed against historical backgrounds, but this serves only to reinforce the idea that it is the novel's distinctive grammar which makes the whole operation work. The novel's reason for existence is to ensure that readers cannot imagine the story it tells otherwise. Whether the novelist needs to check past train timetables, for example, or casualties in a particular battle, depends on the role of fact in the story the novelist wishes to tell. The requirements of the story are paramount. Collingwood is keen to stress that imagination is essential both to the historian and the novelist (the artist whom the historian most resembles: see PH 163). Neither views the past directly, the historian because there is no past to view and the novelist because the story represents nothing beyond the imagination which created it. Content in both history and fiction comes from what is necessary to the story and 'the judge of necessity', as Collingwood says (IH 246), is the imagination itself.

Another resemblance between the novel and history is narrative. Collingwood says less about this than imagination and what he does say seems slight compared with the emphasis which a number of modern philosophers place on narrative as a concept essential not only to history, but to moral philosophy as well. Narrative, as Collingwood understands it, is not simply one of an ensemble of historical techniques. As one of the ways by which historians frame the past, narrative would then take its place alongside key-turning topics such as empire, the family and nationalism. It might compete with the division of history into periods and might sit uncomfortably with history written in terms of abstract formulae such as power or class. But Collingwood does not think of narrative as a technique. As a point of resemblance between history, the novel and music it is too important for that. Thus Collingwood writes that 'in all these cases there is a flow or movement of events, and to understand this is simply to see its continuity, to see how the events flow each into the next' (PH 184). Failure of understanding in history is like failure of understanding in literature or failure of appreciation in music. It is the inability to spot the development in, for example (Collingwood's own: see IH 478), the history of gothic architecture, to see how one phase of construction anticipates the next or how one innovation may be thought of as an improvement. Without the narrative it would be impossible to understand the development, but, more importantly, without the development the sequence of notes in the music, the events in the history or the novel would be mere chronologies, empty of significance. Whether it is a symphony by Brahms, a play by Sophocles or an historical monograph, Collingwood's point is that 'what appears chronologically as a sequence must appear as a simultaneous whole' (IH 478) if each is to be properly understood.

With these two points of resemblance – imagination and narrative – in mind Collingwood is saying that history and the novel are both constructs. Past experience is no more or less than the historian's or the novelist's description of it. Collingwood's commitment is, however, to resemblance, not identity. Certainly, imagination and narrative are basic, but history possesses characteristics that the novel does not need. The most important of these is that 'the historian's picture is meant to be true' (IH 246). The novelist's first duty is to construct a story that makes sense. If the story is art then it must express the emotions the storyteller wishes to express. If it is craft then it must exhibit the skill required to produce its effects. Equally, for Collingwood, the story is told best when it is contrived to speak for itself, when, in other words, the storyteller keeps his own voice out of it, when, as Collingwood says, 'nothing whatever is said about it by the author, and it emerges solely from the incidents and the dialogue' (PH 29). Stories may be told with a high degree of verisimilitude. Thus, a fictional journey through America's Deep South in the years preceding the Civil War may be true to language, time and place. If it is also true to the author's imagination and, if its narrative is compellingly constructed, then readers will follow the story unreservedly, keen to know what happens next. But the appearance of truth is not sufficient to satisfy the historian because narrative in history not only has to make sense; it must also convey, as Collingwood states, 'a picture of things as they really were and of events as they really happened' (IH 246). Collingwood's image of the historian as detective now supersedes his image of the historian as storyteller. For the techniques the detective uses to get at the truth are wholly different from those of the artist wishing to convey the appearance of it. What matters to the historian as detective is not simply the imagination to see how things may have happened and the construction of an intelligible narrative in order to explain why; it is both of these, of course, but it is also a systematic enquiry into the evidence at hand to discover, as far as is practically possible from the standpoint of the present, whether it is tainted, prejudiced, read out of context, mistaken or, in the case of archaeological enquiry, the result of a blundered excavation.

There is one aspect of Collingwood's distinction between the novelist and the historian that we need to look at further. The 'rules of method' (IH 246) establish that history is determinate, self-consistent and related to evidence in ways that works of fiction are not. The second rule states that by contrast with purely imaginary worlds 'there is only one historical world' (IH 246), but what does this mean? Here we must explain Collingwood's intentions in a little more depth. Collingwood's reference is not to the past as a single body of experience – everything that once was. Nor is it to the past as a single body of unalterable experience – everything that once was and cannot be otherwise. Nor is it to the past as a slice of time, something absolutely different from the present and the future. Nor is it to knowledge of the past understood as a single body – everything written by historians. Nor, again, is it to Collingwood's familiar assumption of the rationality of history. We need to remember the context. Collingwood is contrasting purely imaginary worlds with the one historical world. His point, in other words, has to do with the grammar of history. In making up a story writers imagine what characters they please. Moreover, as soon as the characters cease to be imagined they cease to exist. They can be brought into and taken out of existence at the writer's command. But with history it is very different. Once authenticated on the basis of the evidence, an historical event or character cannot be discounted. Historical events stand to each other in determinate ways in the sense that they occur at some definite time and at some particular place. Without this amalgam of temporal and logical sequences, as Collingwood says, 'historical knowledge becomes impossible, for it follows that we can never say about any event "this *must* have happened"; the past can never appear as the conclusion of an historical inference' (IH 110). What is important is that whereas in the imagination there can be many worlds, in the historical imagination (properly exercised in relation to re-enactment and the demands of the evidence) there can only be one. As Collingwood wrote some ten or so years before his Inaugural Lecture, *The Historical Imagination*,

> since a work of art is not asserted as real but only imagined, its existence comes abruptly to an end as soon as we cease to imagine it. The characters in a story which I tell myself only exist for the purposes of the story, and as soon as my story is forgotten they cease to exist and exercise, so to speak, no control over my choice of characters in the next story. Had they been regarded as real characters, I could not thus have ignored them in the next story; for the real must be coherent with itself, and thus history, which aims at narrating real events, can never break off and begin again quite fresh.
>
> (SM 69–70)

To bring the nature of critical history home to us, Collingwood asks us to perform a simple experiment. Herodotus and Thucydides are vital sources for the history of their times. Take a work of nineteenth-century history – say, Grote's massive *History of Greece* – and mark the passages for which there is an original in Herodotus and Thucydides. Collingwood predicts we will find that Grote asks only the questions that the ancient historians asked and is tied to the answers they gave. By contrast, in a modern work such as the

Cambridge Ancient History Collingwood says that we will find historians answering no questions other than their own. In other words, history proper, history as Collingwood understands it, is autonomous and it will not be autonomous unless it is critical.

The historian is centre stage, but even so, the historian is not centre stage as the novelist is. Collingwood says that, unlike the novelist's, 'the historian's picture is meant to be true' (IH 246). It is not true as a mirror to the past, as realism argues. It is true as a critical reconstruction of the past and, yet, this sense is quite sufficient to separate the historical and the fictional worlds. Historians critically re-enact past thought. Novelists do not re-enact their characters' lives at all. The lives of fictional characters must first be enacted in the novelist's imagination and then as the story unfolds. Moreover, the past which the historian re-enacts is never the past as it was actually experienced. The test of completion in history, therefore, is not the repetition of past events but their explanation, and explanation, as Collingwood understands it, is a matter of systematic enquiry in which asking the right questions in the right order is one of the main rules of procedure. By contrast, the test of completion in fiction is nothing but the story. A character's motives may be left hanging or intentions may not be fleshed out, but whether this is a deliberate literary device, a weakness in the writing or simply an oversight can be decided only from the story's own world. It is this thought which lies behind Collingwood's claim that fictional worlds cannot clash. In other words, the differences between history and fiction arise from differences in logical grammar. The actions of Jane Austen's Emma or Conrad's Lord Jim often make us wish to know more about them, and yet it is a wish we can satisfy only by more attentive, possibly more sympathetic readings of the novels in which they appear. Collingwood's point is that we speak about the actions of a Florence Nightingale or an Admiral Lord Nelson differently, since in these cases thoughts are open to historical re-enactment and so it is in principle possible to learn more.

Collingwood claims that the study of history has practical value. Human experience is learned experience, and if it is past experience that we learn from, then history as knowledge of past experience must be embedded in self-knowledge. When human beings learn a language, for example, they do so, Collingwood believes 'by repeatedly and progressively attempting to use it'

(PA 250). Learning from history, however, is not like learning a language for the first time; nor is it like learning a language which is different from the one we already use. Moreover, if Collingwood is right about the gap between history and the novel, then learning from history is not like learning from the novel. In learning from a novel – some feature of human life that is new to us or a combination of motives that we thought impossible – we learn something which only the novel expresses. The novel, in other words, is neither an example nor an exemplar. As with all works of art, we are responding to a world that is unique. We can acquire factual information – say, rates of climate change in the Arctic – from a textbook, a lecture or a computer website. The medium makes no difference. What we acquire is independent of the means by which we acquire it. Similarly, we can grasp a technique by watching someone else displaying it or by following a diagram, but what we grasp is independent of both. With the novel, however, it is different. The novel, says D.H. Lawrence, is 'the one bright book of life'; it enhances life. But it does not enhance life because it is a source of fact or because it is a guide to life. Some novels, as Collingwood goes to great pains to tell us, are not works of art at all. They entertain and distract, but we do not learn from them as we do from art.

Where, then, does this leave learning from history? It is not, we may be sure, a matter of the acquisition of past fact because Collingwood argues that understood as a science of fact history has no existence at all. Nor should we think of history as a guide in the sense of a technique by which later generations learn from earlier ones which decisions to avoid. But neither do we learn from history as we do from art. The novel is an enclosed world. We can deepen our understanding of it, but not learn more. In Collingwood's hands, history is not a technique for getting at past fact. It is rather a model of human understanding. Thus, while we can certainly come to know history better, it is much more important to realize that it is the ways of thought which we use in the process that Collingwood is calling our attention to. Collingwood, in trying to pin down the nature of an historical education, is once again attempting to avoid the twin perils of scientism and romanticism. History is not a source of facts, nor is it a source of laws governing facts. Moreover, it is a romantic fallacy to construe history as art since, as Collingwood writes, 'if history is art, it is at least a very peculiar kind of art. All the artist does is to state what he sees; the historian has both to do this and also to assure himself that what he sees is the truth' (IH 192). Our next concern, then, is the relation between history and practice.

History, politics and progress

Few philosophers of history leave history's value unexamined. Is the historical past merely a collection of relics – a model of Concorde, a fragment from the Berlin Wall, a faded Election Manifesto – each when shorn of its original context totally remote from present concerns? Or is it possible for the historical past to speak to the present? Both questions are philosophical. It may be, as Walter Benjamin remarks, that it is impossible to think of the past, to excavate the remains at Troy or to research the sacking of Carthage, without sadness, but for many philosophers of history, notably those of a liberal persuasion of whom Collingwood should certainly be counted as one, sadness is not the only response. Is history, like nature, an evolutionary process in which natural organisms fight for survival? Or is it the progressive realization of human freedom? Or, is it, as Collingwood thought, neither of these, but rather a form of thinking which makes human beings what they are?

Learning presupposes an organized body of experience from which to learn. Learning how to ride a bike, play chess, tie knots, take examinations, conduct experiments are all activities in which a debt to the past must be paid. Learning that something is the case similarly presupposes the existence of a body of verified fact or a method of inquiry for discovering the facts. It is tempting, therefore, to think of learning from history in the same light. To learn from it, history must be expressible as an organized body of experience or as a body of verifiable fact. History as an arbitrary jumble of events can teach us nothing, but history as a story which manifests a plot is something from which it is possible to learn. Find the key to history and we can learn from it. As with nature, leave history blind and it remains lawless, a state from which we can learn nothing.

Many philosophers of history have understood history's value in this way, but Collingwood is not one of them. Indeed, Collingwood makes it absolutely plain, first, that there is no analogy between history and nature and, second, that there is no pattern to history. And, yet, Collingwood not only retains the belief that history has value; he stresses the impossibility of action without it. History and practice bear the closest possible relation, but how can this be if there is no pattern in history from which we can learn? To tease out Collingwood's own position we must examine his criticisms: first, of the theory of evolution as applied to history and second of the idea of universal history. Darwinism and speculative philosophy of history provide Collingwood with different targets to aim at, and in formulating his own views on the value of history he states what he believes is true and false in each.

Darwinism is a theory of natural selection rather than of history, but it has an application to human development and so to the changes which occur in a human life over time. Collingwood is, in general terms, an admirer of Darwin, but not of Darwinism. To understand human activities solely on the model of nature is to commit a category mistake, and, yet, outside *The Idea of History*, as early as 1924, Collingwood was spelling out his own attitude by describing evolution and progress as 'only half-understood and mythological expressions of the concept of history' (SM 54). 'Half-understood' because Darwin does see that nature evolves over time and is not a static system. 'Mythological' because Darwinism replaces the complexities of historical development with a single idea, the myth of natural selection. In the Darwinian picture natural and historical processes exhibit change over time, opening the way to seeing both as governed by the same criteria. Collingwood writes: 'evolution could now be used as a generic term covering both historical progress and natural progress' (IH 129). To call a natural process evolutionary is to say a lot more than that events in nature repeat themselves or even that new forms come into existence by modifying old ones. It is to say that an evolutionary process must be progressive because new forms not only supersede old ones; they do so in a specific order in which, as Collingwood comments, 'each new form is not only a modification of the last, but an improvement on it' (IH 321).

As applied to human history, what Darwinism teaches primarily is that progress comes about as a law of nature and that historical and natural processes are governed by the same laws. As in nature, new forms of social and political existence must necessarily supplant their predecessors. On Collingwood's view, Darwinism as a theory of history is right to see the historical process as a process of change, possibly even as struggle, but wrong to see it as changing on the model of nature. Progress in history, therefore, whatever it is, is not like progress in nature as Darwin conceives it, since, as Collingwood points out in a destructive passage,

> The conception of a 'law of progress', by which the course of history is so governed that successive forms of human activity exhibit each an improvement on the last, is thus a mere confusion of thought, bred of an unnatural union between man's belief in his own superiority to nature and his belief that he is nothing more than a part of nature. If either belief is true, the other is false: they cannot be combined to produce logical offspring.
>
> (IH 323)

We should be clear that Collingwood's aim is not to deny the possibility of human progress, but to rescue it. He is saying that if history is understood as analogous to nature then progress does not make sense. In neither history nor nature is change merely the repetition of types – in pointing to this, Darwin was right, but human history stands alone because it concerns actions, and actions become properly historical only when they are made the subject of historical re-enactment. Thus, Collingwood writes: 'no succession of events is an historical succession unless it consists of acts whose motives can, in principle at least, be thus re-enacted' (IH 115). In other words, unlike natural processes which operate according to their own internal logic, the historical process is one in which the historian has a central role. Whereas Darwinian scientists do not need to think of themselves as participants in the events they describe, the historian, by contrast, is the key to the past coming alive at all.

Re-enactment gives us a significant clue to Collingwood's own views on historical progress, but before following these up we need to consider our second false trail. We may think that Collingwood, as a liberal political philosopher, should be sympathetic to an idea embedded in liberalism since the eighteenth century that history is not only patterned but also progressive. Universal history, as the child of speculative philosophy and philosophical history, is a necessary expression of the rational essence of humanity in its temporal aspect. Thus, in the hands of a figure of the Enlightenment such as Kant, history is progressive because in the completion of rational human freedom it possesses a determinate goal.

In his discussion of Kant (IH 93–104) Collingwood goes to some lengths to stress the confusion which results when the progressiveness of history is linked too closely with the picture of history as the sequential evolution of events. The key difference between the Kantian and the evolutionary view is that for Kant (and for Collingwood, too) the progressiveness of history has no parallel in nature. So, as Collingwood remarks, we encounter the eighteenth-century thought that 'a human society in which there was no progress in rationality would be a society without a history, like the non-historical or merely natural societies of bees or ants' (IH 99). In other words, once history is separated from nature it makes sense to ask why a human society progresses rather than stagnates, and what makes this progress happen.

And, yet, ambitions for a universal history leave Collingwood unconvinced, since Kant's distinctions between universal history and particular, between reason and passion and intelligence and ignorance are, in Collingwood's view, too rigid. Moreover, if history is progressive it is not because there is a pattern in human nature which makes it so. Universal history in Kant's picture of it fails because, as Collingwood points out, history ends, not at a pre-determined future point, but, much more prosaically, in the present. Thus, Collingwood comments, 'the historian's task is to show how the present has come into existence; he cannot show how the future will come into existence, for he does not know what the future will be' (IH 104). That Collingwood owes a great deal to Kant in his general philosophical approach to the nature of historical knowledge is clear. One writer on Collingwood remarks:

> in an argumentative strategy that closely resembles Kant's defence of *a priori* categories, Collingwood claims that what enables historians to distinguish between historical and non-historical human deeds has to do with the fact that they bring certain presuppositions to the investigation of the material.
>
> (Giuseppina D'Oro. (2002), *Collingwood and the Metaphysics of Experience*, London: Routledge, 106)

Philosophy, in other words, asks what makes historical knowledge possible and it answers by identifying the concepts which belong specifically to history as an autonomous mode of enquiry. Collingwood's revolution in history and the historiographical consequences which flow from it derive their force from this methodological starting point. However, a philosophy which imposes itself upon history, as Collingwood believed Kant's did, will result only in a flawed picture of the goodness and badness which the history of human actions displays. Thus, Collingwood writes:

> this exaggerated division of history into a wholly irrational past and a wholly rational future is the legacy which Kant inherits from the Enlightenment. A profounder knowledge of history would have taught him that what has brought progress about has not been the sheer ignorance or the sheer badness but the concrete actuality of human effort itself, with all its good and bad elements commingled.
>
> (IH 102; see Dray (1995, 116) for discussion)

In linking human reason with human history Collingwood thought that Kant 'achieved the remarkable feat of showing why there should be such a thing as history' (IH 98), but that is as far as the affinity goes. For by denying that the historian has no business with the future Collingwood at a stroke separates history proper from all forms of historical forecasting. The future has no witnesses, there is no evidence for it and, for the obvious reason that what has not yet happened cannot be re-enacted, is itself firmly closed to historical interest. However, we should not conclude from this that Collingwood confines the historian to wholly less speculative business. Quite the contrary, in fact, since Collingwood's remarks on Schiller credit him with the ability to 'detect the large-scale rhythms of the historical process' (IH 105) and with the insight to see that history as the story of humanity from its 'savage beginnings to modern civilization' (IH 105) ends not in the future but in the present, and then not only in present political institutions but also in the art, religion and economics of the present as well.

The setting for Collingwood's own views on the value of history is his humane Hegelianism. Indeed, the titles of two of his main essays on this subject – 'History and Freedom' (IH 315–20) and 'Progress as Created by Historical Thinking' (IH 321–34) – are strong indications of their origins. Indebtedness is no guarantee of discipleship, however. Collingwood's opinions are distinctive, and he defends them by his own arguments and in his own characteristic manner. The truths in Hegel (IH 113–22) are the refusal to discuss history by analogy with nature, the determination to understand history as the history of thought and the idea that the mainspring of history is reason. Despite these advances the claim that logic is the clue to history is, for Collingwood, a step too far. Hegel had argued that if there is a pattern to history it comes not from fact but from ideas. Moreover, if ideas have a logical structure then the passage of time is not simply a matter of chronology, but of one movement of thought shading necessarily into its successor. Collingwood, however, is not convinced. Grounding history in logic contains one fatal flaw. No pattern imputed to history will be credible unless it is based on evidence. To assume without evidence that one historical period must be of a certain type or possess specific attributes or to have more significance in the development of a given idea than any other is to set history (at least as Collingwood understands it) aside.

Universal history, then, has little appeal for Collingwood. There can be no history of everything: 'all history is the history of something, something definite and particular', Collingwood writes ('The Philosophy of Progress', 1929, Debbins, 1965, 130) in a phrase which does not make the problem of progress in history any easier for him to solve. For if history is to be seen as progressive, a transition from a worse state to a better one (as opposed to regressive, a transition from a better state to a worse one), then we need a criterion of judgement to decide what is to count as improvement and what is not. Moreover, since all human societies exist in time any criterion will also be the standpoint of a given society at a particular stage of its history. When we remember that Collingwood has already rejected the idea that there is some natural law or conceptual pattern to history which allows progress to be traced, if not indisputably established, then his difficulty becomes obvious. It seems then that as a liberal, Collingwood has succeeded only in sawing off the branch he is sitting on. For if history exhibits no pattern and if there is no view from Olympus to assess human development, then progress is beyond human calculation.

Collingwood tackles these difficulties by means of an example (IH 324–7), one that is made up, but not wholly alien. Imagine a community of fish eaters who, with their fish supply failing, seek food by digging for roots. A change has occurred both in their situation and in their activities, but we should not think of this as progress because progress suggests improvement, and there is nothing in the new way of obtaining food which makes it better than the old. If, however, the same community could improve the efficiency of their fishing methods so that both their catch and their labour saving increased, then we should consider this to be progress. Working less and catching more fish is better than working harder and catching fewer fish. But Collingwood points out that it belongs to the concept of progress that it may be seen in different ways. From the perspective of the new generation of fish eaters the change to more efficient methods is a change for the better. For the old, however, seeing no need for their way of life to alter and accustomed to the institutions and values which have built up around it, not wanting the increased leisure which results from greater efficiency, the new methods are not only unnecessary but a step backward. What makes life better from the viewpoint of one generation makes it worse from the viewpoint of another.

To overcome inter-generational myopia Collingwood turns to history. Indeed, Collingwood's own account of historical progress follows closely from his understanding of the subject matter of history and his doctrine of historical re-enactment. From the former Collingwood derives the argument that as there can be no history of nature there can be no progress in nature either. The instincts, appetites and desires of human beings arise from a biological not an historical environment; moreover, desires, as functions of the individuals who pursue them, are closed to interpersonal comparison. So when Collingwood remarks that 'the happiness of a peasant is not contained in the happiness of a millionaire' (IH 330) we may reasonably infer a strong resistance to a utilitarian criterion of progress. From the latter – the doctrine of re-enactment – Collingwood argues more positively that for progress to be spoken of at all we must not only be able to judge one generation's way of life better than the lives of its predecessors, but also make such a judgement from a standpoint separate from that of the generations concerned. It is history itself which is the standpoint Collingwood is seeking. Any estimation of progress is possible only on condition of knowing what the old way of life was like, that is, having historical knowledge of his society's past while he is living in the present he is creating: for historical knowledge is simply the re-enactment of past experience in the mind of the present thinker.

(IH 326)

At this point the question we need to ask becomes obvious. Re-enactment by itself is no indicator of progress. Re-enactment enables a comparison between one way of life and another, but it does not tell us whether one is better than the other. Thus Collingwood needs an additional argument. Where, then, does he find it? After some cautionary advice concerning the difficulties of making historical judgements about the relative value of different ways of life and some warnings about the illusions that can be generated by labelling historical periods 'good' or 'bad', 'enlightened' or 'superstitious', Collingwood turns to progress properly understood. Progress properly understood must first be history properly understood; that is, whether one historical period or way of life represents progress over another can be decided only after both have been grasped historically by the historian sympathetically reconstructing both and ensuring that no defect in re-enactment has blurred his account of their values. Second, the historian has to reach an estimation of the value of one period or way of life compared with another. This cannot be achieved, however, by assuming that the subjects to be compared aim at the same goal so that one may be judged better at reaching it. As Collingwood remarks, 'Bach was not trying to write like Beethoven and failing; Athens was not a relatively unsuccessful attempt to produce Rome; Plato was himself, not a half-developed Aristotle' (IH 329). Each form of life is to be judged in terms of the problems it sets itself. But re-enactment would be impossible in the absence of the present experience of the historian and, since the present has standards of its own, an independent criterion is required. Collingwood says that the question of progress can be settled only by the following process of assessment. Here we need to quote at length:

If thought in its first phase, after solving the initial problems of that phase, is then, through solving these, brought up against others which defeat it; and if the second solves these further problems without losing its hold on the solution of the first, so that there is gain without any corresponding loss, then there is progress. And there can be progress on no other terms. If there is any loss, the problem of setting loss against gain is insoluble.

(IH 329)

We can assess Collingwood's account of progress: first, in terms of the assumptions he brings to it, and second, in terms of the proposed criterion itself. Collingwood assumes that progress must be understood primarily as history. Thus, what counts as history's subject matter also counts for or against our considering an historical period, a way of life or a specific development as progress. By the same token, what is not the subject matter of history can play no part in any estimation of progress. What is closed to historical knowledge is, in Collingwood's view, closed in two ways. First, where there is no evidence there is nothing to re-enact and so historical knowledge is impossible. Thus, where the past cannot be known (in Collingwood's sense of known), no judgement of it as progressive or not is possible. Indeed, Collingwood speaks often of the impossibility of knowing (and, hence, evaluating as progressive or not) historical periods in their entirety. As historical knowledge is selective, Collingwood is wary of accounts of progress which stem from historical laws or law-like generalizations about the past. Second, where the past exists only as feelings and desires, we can have no knowledge of it because feelings and desires cannot be re-enacted. Thus, there can be no such thing as material progress because this depends upon the increased satisfaction of appetites and desires and, equally, there can be no such thing as artistic progress because the work of art expresses the feelings of the artist and these are unique to the individual concerned. The first sense in which history is closed is contingent because new evidence is always possible. The second sense is necessary because it is conceptually impossible to re-enact the feelings of past individuals. It is, therefore, never possible to evaluate past feelings – what was felt and the degree to which it was felt – as progressive or not. So to the extent that moral life depends on unreflective experience it cannot exhibit progress. In any estimation of progress, on Collingwood's account, therefore, the feelings, appetites, instincts and desires of past human beings simply do not come into it.

The problem of progress is, for Collingwood, primarily an intellectual one. This does not mean, however, that a given mode of thought is able to set a standard for progress which all other modes of thought must meet. So Collingwood does not think of scientific progress as in any sense paradigmatic. Like progress in philosophy, in the institutions of moral, economic and political life and in religion, science has its own criterion of appropriateness. Progress in philosophy, for example, is not a matter of verification whereas progress in science conspicuously is. And, yet, Collingwood's own criterion for the assessment of progress is a general one. Progress in solving scientific problems involves the standards, methods and procedures that are specific to science, but the general requirement for progress, that there should be gain without any corresponding loss, is applicable to all.

How adequate, then, is Collingwood's proposed criterion for progress? We might think first of all that Collingwood had almost designed his understanding of progress deliberately to counter utilitarianism, since it contains no sense at all in which progress can apply to anything other than unqualified goods. The calculation of gain against loss which is the utilitarian's stock in trade has no role here. For example, changes in air travel which allow greater numbers of people to move more quickly over greater distances at reduced cost may for the utilitarian be progress, even though negative consequences such as increased environmental damage invariably accompany them. But for Collingwood they would surely not. Collingwood's proposed criterion is certainly narrow, but it is not necessarily conservative for that. When we read *The Idea of History* we see clearly that progress is explained in terms of problem solving. Thus, for example, when playing chess, progress is marked not by taking two pawns and losing one, but by solving the problem of how to protect my bishop without imperiling my ability to launch a queen side attack. It is a feature of progress that it opens up possibilities for the future rather than just delivering an immediate advantage, however substantial that may be. So, on Collingwood's understanding, we can think of the abolition of slavery in the nineteenth-century American Southern States as progress because it brought that society closer to the moral ideal, even though many slave owners were greatly pained by it, and, as Collingwood remarks, 'it was a good act to abolish slavery, but the men who are born into a slaveless world are not automatically made good men by that fact' (Debbins, 1965, 115). As long as the problems created by abolition are solved without a return to the injustices which led to them, we can speak of progress. Historical knowledge enters through the determination to eliminate the evils of the past, but abolition was motivated as much by hopes for the future, which suggests at least one dimension to progress that is outside the historian's concern.

Collingwood's discussion of progress is important because it illustrates the sense in which moral and political problems are necessarily temporal. There is little in Collingwood's writings to suggest that progress is an irresistible tide crushing all those who stand in its path. Equally, there is little to suggest that he thinks of progress as something totally open to individual choice. In Collingwood's fishing community example individuals do not choose the generation they belong to, but they do find it hard to understand and sympathize with earlier ways of life, and they wish to make changes to their own way of living which may well require others to make sacrifices. Clearly, progress is not wholly concerned with resources, but how resources are distributed between individuals within one generation and between genera-tions is a matter that no discussion of progress can ignore. Here, we might reasonably conclude, is an area where the philosophy of history and political philosophy are closely linked. Since one of Collingwood's overriding interests was the bearing of history upon politics we should give a little more thought to it.

Generations stand to each other necessarily in time. They are ordered temporally, each related to preceding generations as successor and to those following as predecessor. What counts as progress between generations, therefore, will be shaped by the sequential relations that bind them together. Since these are historical relations we should expect Collingwood to say something about them, and he does. In the course of defending a non-causal theory of action (IH 474–5), Collingwood argues that thoughts make up a sequence, each setting the context for the next and so on. A chess player (this time Collingwood's example, not mine) makes his own move, and in doing so both responds to his opponent and creates a new situation for his opponent to ponder. Historical sequences take this as their model, each action standing non-causally to the other. In the chess example, however, the freedom to move one way or the other is dependent on accepting the authority of the rules of chess. Historical sequences are both rule-governed and expressive of freedom, but the rules change over time, and so, as Collingwood writes, 'it is the task of the historian to discover what principles guided the actions of the persons he is studying, and not to assume that these have always been the same' (IH 475). Now there is at least one sense in which relations between generations must be the same. Unlike relations between contemporaries relations between generations are not symmetrical. Since time flows one way a generation can benefit or harm its remote successors, but not expect benefit or harm in return. Between contemporaries, there can be reciprocity. In relations between one generation and those that follow it a long way down the line there cannot.

As Collingwood realizes (IH 331), none of this is as abstruse as it sounds. Our saving and investment have consequences for the individuals who follow. Our consumption of scarce resources has effects for the future. Some damage to the environment may only be noticeable in the long term. If we have nothing to fear from future generations then, on at least one theory of obligation, apart from our immediate successors, we have little reason to take the future into account. Since Collingwood's political philosophy lacks a theory of social justice (he does not try to develop a theory of inter-generational justice along, say, the lines made famous by John Rawls), we might expect his theory of progress to do some work in this direction.

In Collingwood's hands progress is a special case of re-enactment. Newtonian science lives on in Einstein, 'but re-enacted here and now together with a development of itself that is partly constructive or positive and partly critical or negative' (IH 334). When we add to this Collingwood's thought that the past remains encapsulated in the present in the form of evidence, it is reasonable to assume that Collingwood thinks of historical generations as overlapping. Of course, in one obvious sense all generations overlap because each single generation shares the scene with its immediate predecessors and successors, but Collingwood's point is broader. Historical re-enactment dependent on the evidence concerns the past and it is important because it counters the 'optical illusion' (IH 328) of taking the present as the litmus test of the past.

Thus, when we return to the community of fish eaters, Collingwood is surely right to argue that without historical knowledge of past food-gathering practices any estimation of new methods would be impossible. However, Collingwood's proposed criterion for progress, that there should be gain without any corresponding loss, is less persuasive. What is progress for the present generation may come at a high price for the future as when, for example, new fishing methods stimulate consumption to the point where resources are seriously depleted. As Collingwood acknowledges, present decisions create problems for future generations to solve. But Collingwood does not see past, present and future generations as related in terms of justice; nor does he see history as necessarily enlightened so that the present generation can ignore its problems, confident that in the future they will be solved. Ignorance of the future (one of the boundaries of history as Collingwood understands it) cuts both ways and this surely means that as far as Collingwood's criterion for progress is concerned, although Collingwood's philosophy of history has said a great deal and taken his argument so far, political philosophy still has a lot more to say.

Before we leave Collingwood's discussion, there is one final difficulty we need to examine. Collingwood's sharp separation of history from nature excludes human instincts, appetites and feelings from history. But it is important to notice that Collingwood does not think of human beings as reasoning machines. He writes: 'the idea that man, apart from his self-conscious historical life, is different from the rest of creation in being a rational animal is mere superstition' (IH 227). We have already seen that Collingwood's remark gives no support to the claim that human feelings can be made the subject of historical knowledge. As Collingwood comments himself, 'so long as man's conduct is determined by what may be called his animal nature, it is non-historical: the process of those activities is a natural process' (IH 216). We can think of learning how to avoid mistakes in chess as a reasonable expression of Collingwood's view that progress is a matter of solving intellectual problems cumulatively. Chess players learn that dominating the centre of the board is an essential strategy and that placing major pieces in the line of fire behind minor ones is likely to lead to trouble. Learning from history, however, is different because mistakes in history are different. In history human passions such as pride, jealousy and avarice, for example, are as much involved in events as human thought. Human sentiments are as much involved in decisions as calculation and planning. Collingwood's exclusion clause now begins to look arbitrary. Moreover, it would surely make learning from history impossible.

Collingwood's difficulty arises from his insistence that understanding human conduct is conceptually distinct from understanding animal behaviour. Human beings are unique in their awareness of their own activities. Human conduct is reflexive. Spiders spin, but they do not act. Dolphins search for food, but they do not hunt. Gorillas mate, but they do not express their feelings in romantic poetry. The spider's web is intricate, purpose-built and constructed over time, but it has no history. History, as Collingwood understands it, is autonomous. Take away thought and knowledge of the past vanishes. And, yet, Collingwood does not think of human beings solely as reasoning creatures. Past thought, however, is open to re-enactment whereas feelings are not. Re-enactment is one of the essential conditions of historical knowledge and so Collingwood's unwillingness to include human nature in human history is more understandable. The price Collingwood pays is the narrowing of history's subject-matter and, hence, the imposition of limits on what may be learned from history and how.

There is, however, an escape route. The price need not be paid if Collingwood can reconnect nature with thought. Instinct, appetites and feelings by themselves are not subjects of historical knowledge. Thus Collingwood writes: 'it makes no difference to the historian, as an historian, that there should be no food in a poor man's house' (IH 315), but when food shortage is presented not as the physiological expression of hunger, but as the reason for it, in the form, say, of institutional failings, then the historian can go to work. On this basis, therefore, it is open to Collingwood to include human feelings within the range of re-enactment, but only so long as they can be expressed as thought. It is not only defenders of cognitive accounts of the feelings who will be pleased by this conclusion. Defenders of Collingwood who wish to resist the charge that he confines history to intellectual history will also want to celebrate.

However, when we consider the idea of a history of non-human animals Collingwood's overall view is to reject it, even though there are a few favourable concessionary hints on the margins of his main theory. Thus, supporters of the claim that differences between human and non-human animals are differences of degree will find something to ponder when Collingwood argues that cats taught washing by their mothers display 'the beginnings of historical life' (IH 227). And, yet, we should be clear that history in the sense that Collingwood understands it is quite distant from the rudimentary manifestations of it in some non-human animal behaviour. When Collingwood speaks about non-human animals outside *The Idea of History* it is usually to stress just how inconceivable it is to think of their behaviour in terms of thoughts and arguments. So we find him writing:

> everyone knows that dogs chase cats because cats run away; the cat's exhibition of fear produces in the dog, not an argument running thus: 'this cat is afraid of me; it evidently thinks I can kill it, so I suppose I can; here goes', but an immediate response in the shape of aggressive emotion.
>
> (PA 231)

The difference between human and non-human animal behaviour is one of kind, and so the learning from the past displayed when a kitten learns from its mother is a rudiment of history only in the sense of being an imperfect indication of it. Collingwood issues a similar warning against attempts to think of non-human animal life historically when he speaks of trying to interpret their behaviour from the evidence they leave, say, habitat, tracks or of migratory movements (PH 77). The ever-present danger here is anthropomorphism. In human conduct the questions which historians ask of the evidence are necessarily related to a conception of human life and what it involves. So whereas it makes perfect sense to ask what conception of history was held by the ancient Sumerians, or whether or not they held one at all (IH 12), the question of a non-human animal sense of history is entirely a conceptual one. Does it make sense, for example, to think of dogs celebrating the anniversary of the Battle of Waterloo because a canine ancestor played a part in it? Or of pigs celebrating their escape from the lorry which overturned on its way to the abattoir? (Here we are surely in the world of Orwell's *Animal Farm*, as opposed to history as Collingwood understands it.)

Collingwood sometimes speaks of progress in a more conventional liberal fashion. Thus, the modern liberal state in its capacity to enhance as well as protect human freedoms is 'one of the most certain proofs of human progress' ('A Philosophy of Progress',

1929, Debbins, 1965, 120). But if this is so, it is not because of history itself or because liberals are necessarily travelling in the right direction. It is of the essence of Collingwood's discussion that he sees progress as the result of human choice and effort. Certainly, without the ability to critically re-enact what has gone before, no advancement would be possible. But what instigates the advancement is the will and determination of specific historical agents to act for the better. The concept of progress is, therefore, a link between Collingwood's philosophy of history and his political philosophy, most especially his treatment of civilization in *The New Leviathan* (1942).

CHAPTER FIVE

Receptions and Reactions

Reception

The Idea of History first appeared in 1946, some three years after Collingwood's death, and was widely and appreciatively reviewed. No doubt Collingwood's academic reputation played a part in this, but the nature of history itself following the Second World War was as much a topic of interest and concern as it was after the First World War. A War had just ended which had shaken liberal assumptions about civilization to their core. Collingwood attempted to restate liberalism for dark times in his *The New Leviathan* (1942) and so it is not surprising, perhaps, that liberals should look to *The Idea of History* for a source of hope. For what Collingwood taught was that the past could not be forcibly retold to serve political ends. A liberal society's history is as important to it as its democratic rights and duties. Moreover, as philosophy is able to demonstrate, history is both autonomous and systematic. By making human thought and action its central focus, liberal historiography parallels liberal political philosophy. In both it is the individual who is the basic subject. Action is a concept that is fundamental to Collingwood's philosophy of history and to his political philosophy. Understanding human conduct is different from explaining natural phenomena. Neither history nor politics can be adequately grasped from the perspective of natural science.

And, yet, without philosophical exposition and defence Collingwood's liberal ideals are surely no more than pieties. Here we need to appreciate just how distant Collingwood's own philosophical approach was from the post-war intellectual mood. First, the realism which Collingwood attacked so fiercely was far from dead. The problem of historical knowledge remained that of establishing its autonomy if it could not be constructed on the model of natural science. Second, the linguistic philosophy predominant at the time had the effect of turning the philosophy of history into the philosophy of language. The job of philosophy is to analyse the statements we make about the world. Thus, philosophers of history are directed to temporal statements and the kind of logic they exhibit. Collingwood's treatment of history is by no means uninterested in this, but it is not its exclusive concern. Third, contemporary moral and political philosophy was not untouched by the prevailing shift to the investigation of language. Collingwood's attempt to bring philosophy closer to life was as a result made to appear moralistic and the Kantian origins of his attempt to show how history was possible almost completely neglected. Collingwood's overriding aim was to bring philosophy, history and practice together and if the result was not as theoretically sealed as it appeared, it was still too much of a 'grand synthesis' for a world that had largely turned away from the Hegelian origins of Collingwood's thought.

It has to be said, too, that the early reception of *The Idea of History* was often marked by misunderstanding. To take one example of many: during an Aristotelian Society symposium held in Cambridge in July 1947 A. M. MacIver, in the course of criticizing Collingwood's doctrine that all history is contemporary history, commented that what made historical experience came not from 'twentieth-century Oxford or Cambridge college rooms', but in the case of the Peloponnesian War, 'the experiences of thousands of poor devils two dozen centuries ago' (PAS, Supp. Vol. XXI, 1947, 33), as if Collingwood was denying this. Not a few early readers of *The Idea of History* confused what made history possible with what history was about.

A quite different kind of early misunderstanding requires a little more attention. A number of Collingwood's first reviewers noted the way in which *The Idea of History* had been put together, the

American philosopher, Arthur E. Murphy, calling it 'something of a patchwork', and Michael Oakeshott, in *The English Historical Review*, referring to it as 'unfinished and scrappy'. Neither felt that this undermined the work's undoubted philosophical merits, but it is true that the book's original form of publication influenced the ways in which Collingwood's views were first understood. As the revised edition of *The Idea of History* (1994) and the publication of *The Principles of History* (1999) demonstrate, we now have Collingwood's philosophy of history in all its many aspects in as comprehensive a form as we are likely to get. Even so, Collingwood's first reviewers were in no position to know exactly how much unpublished material lay behind *The Idea of History* as it appeared to them in 1946. Apart from expressing their confidence that Collingwood's work would be a seminal text in the philosophy of history few, if any, would have been able to anticipate the way Collingwood's writings slipped into the philosophical shadows in the 1950s, enjoyed a period of immense reinterpretation and resuscitation in the 1960s and 1970s and, with the availability of Collingwood's unpublished manuscripts after 1978, and the discovery of the lost manuscript of *The Principles of History* in 1995, appear in the comprehensive versions that are read today. Under the guidance of the editor T. M. Knox, the first reviewers were aware that *The Idea of History* was not the work that Collingwood intended, but overall they read the book plainly for its philosophical views, and if their first impressions often left a great deal unsaid or said wrongly, they do highlight a number of topics which take us to the heart of what Collingwood wants to say. My aim here is to treat four of Collingwood's first reviewers as fellow conversationalists and critics. I will take each as adopting a particular standpoint on a specific topic, and allow each to present their case and then comment on what they have to say. *The Idea of History* was published posthumously. It contains work written at different times and often for different purposes. Moreover (and under the influence of Knox's Introduction), on topics as central as the relation between philosophy and history, for example, Collingwood may be read (and, as we shall see, often was) as defending positions which seem flatly to contradict arguments he put forward in other major books and papers. Much of the renaissance in Collingwood studies came about because it was felt that that this disunity gave a wholly false impression of Collingwood's philosophical method and purpose. Thus, a great deal of valuable work was done in order to demonstrate the overall coherence of Collingwood's writings. On this basis *The Idea of History* is to be seen not as an afterword, parts of which were written in its author's decline, but, when separated into its component elements, a record of thinking on history which may be shown to be in complete harmony with his views elsewhere. Arguments about the success of this long-term revisionary project continue, but they are not my concern here. My aim is to act as a guide for readers of just one of the texts which make up the corpus of Collingwood's philosophical writing. Like Collingwood's first reviewers I have a specific focus, but, unlike them, I am not bound by the conventions of reviewing. Thus, where the reviewer touches on a problem we are in a position to force the issue; where a skirmish is threatened we can start a battle. Reviews are not, of course, full-scale critical discussions but they are first impressions and as such, even when they are only hints of arguments as opposed to arguments themselves, they are worth taking up and considering further.

Reviews

Commonsense views of history found their champion in the American anthropologist J. S. Slotkin, who in 1948 reviewed *The Idea of History* for *Antiquity*, a journal to which Collingwood himself contributed a number of articles and reviews (*Antiquity*, 22, 98–102). Collingwood's reviewer argued that history, far from being autonomous, is, in fact, modelled on science. Historians faced with the problem of accounting for a past event – say, the French Revolution – work no less than scientists from the facts available to them. Certainly, facts come alive through hypothesis and interpretation, but without laws and generalizations held to be true, hypothesis and interpretation have no testable basis, so when the historian infers that such and such must be true because it is the only account which fits the evidence it is the law or generalization implied in the claim that is doing the work. Laws or generalizations 'which have been verified by comparative and experimental method' (Slotkin, 1948, 100) form the bedrock of historical method. Without them it would be impossible to assess rival accounts of past events and to judge a given historical account as true. Thus, at least one of Collingwood's early readers left *The Idea of History* unconvinced. History is not autonomous at all. It works like science. Laws accepted as true provide the test for new hypotheses and explanations. Thus, Collingwood's reviewer writes,

> The human historian observes an artifact such as a manuscript and makes certain inferences about the Peloponnesian war; the physicist observes rings on a metal foil and makes certain inferences about the atomic conditions which produced them. If anyone doubts either inference he can go to the facts and form his own conclusions. The facts for the human historian are material objects from the past (artifacts) and living people's observations (their memories of past observations and their present observations in the case of contemporary history). The facts for the scientist are likewise objects (remains of past events) and living scientists' observations (their memories of past observations and their present observations).
>
> (Slotkin, 1948, 101)

The past, in other words, is as much a laboratory as the present. Sever the link between history and science and the connection between history and certainty is lost. Why did the French Revolution occur when it did? What caused it to occur? Why did it happen? Questions such as these are the historian's meat and drink, but to the common sense mind no answer will be in any way credible unless it meets or approximates to criteria set by science. In this early review the voice of realism is unmistakable, but the scorpion is also hard at work, since there is also a sting in the tale. Thus the review not only accuses Collingwood of getting history wrong; it also accuses him of disguising history's dependence on science. Thus, when Collingwood thinks he is describing a genuinely historical inference, he is, either explicitly or implicitly, making an appeal to science because it is generalization which makes the inference possible. Collingwood made it his general practice not to reply to reviewers, but we can. Is the separation of history and science in Collingwood's philosophy of history complete, or is there room for laws and law-like generalizations? Much of the early reception of *The Idea of History* concerns these issues and so we should give them our attention.

The reception of Collingwood's philosophy of history by positivism tells us just how strongly his views ran against the tide. Collingwood argues that to understand a past action it is necessary to grasp the thought behind it. But for philosophers of science, such as C.G. Hempel, explanation requires not only the correct ascription of a specific thought but also the establishment of a valid connection between the thought and the action which follows from it. Moreover, this is possible only if it is known that in general, thoughts of a specific type result in actions of a specific type. Without the law or the law-like generalization we would never know whether the object to be explained occurred by chance. We would not be able to see the necessity of it. From this point of view there is simply no difference in explaining actions and events. With equal force there is also no difference between explaining past actions and events and present ones. Actions are to be explained by connecting them to their necessary antecedent conditions. Motives and intentions (specific forms of Collingwood's thoughts behind the actions) are important in history only if they can be located in some more general causal matrix.

During the 1950s and early 1960s the reception of *The Idea of History* was largely shaped by prevailing debates over the possibility of the human sciences being modelled on the assumptions and procedures of natural science. What was distinctive in Collingwood's philosophy of history – the doctrine of re-enactment, the historical imagination and the nature of historical evidence – was generally thought significant only to the extent that it could be used as argument for or (more usually) against the idea of a social science. In this context Collingwood's specific concern with historical knowledge was often ignored or treated as less important than his views about the nature of human understanding in general. From Collingwood's point of view a reception such as this would have to be seen as a setback to what he was trying to achieve because the indispensability of history to human understanding in general is precisely what *The Idea of History* is about. Thus, any move towards rescuing Collingwood from debates over the nature of social science should also serve to reinstate his primary concern with history as a mode of human experience and understanding. Thus by highlighting what is wrong with the early responses to Collingwood on the nature of scientific history, we are, in effect, engaging with the

history of his views on history and, in the process, returning those
views to centre stage.

Collingwood does accept that the point of an explanation
in science – of why a volcano erupts or a star system explodes
– is to indicate the necessity of what occurred, but in the case
of natural phenomena the scientist in knowing what happened
does not always know why it did; hence the need for conjecture,
observation, experiment and proof. The historian, by contrast, in
knowing what happened also knows why. There is, in other words,
a fundamental difference between explaining an event in nature
and understanding human conduct. Re-enactment is Collingwood's
way of marking this difference. Thus, whereas the scientist is driven
to explanations which operate from the outside by subsuming
the events to be explained under the relevant laws, the historian
has no such need. Once the historian has ascertained the nature
of a past fact (by rethinking the thought it involves) then, as
Collingwood writes, 'nothing of value is left for generalization to
do' (IH 223). We can illustrate what Collingwood means by one of
his own examples. Once the historian has grasped why Napoleon
established his domination of post-revolutionary France then, as
Collingwood says, 'nothing is added to our understanding of that
process by the statement (however true) that similar things have
happened elsewhere' (IH 223).

Generalization, as Collingwood acknowledges, can be useful in
history where a particular event is resistant to understanding on
its own, but since the object of historical knowledge is to capture
the past in its full individuality, then his intention is surely to push
generalization to the margins. A generalization aims to explain one
event by connecting it in a significant way with others, but, for
Collingwood, there is no guarantee that what is considered causally
significant in one historical period will be repeated by later ones
(IH 223–4). Thus, what is presented as an 'iron law' of historical
events is not so much a law as the manifestation of a given set of
particular assumptions and predispositions. While the precise role
of generalization in historical understanding remains very much
alive in contemporary discussion of Collingwood, his own view
is to minimize it. So even though Collingwood does allow the
historian to deploy generalizations he confines these to explanations in which natural events impinge upon human practices, most
obviously in the cases of the environment and disease. It is worth

remarking that Collingwood does use generalizations in his own archaeological work rather than in his theorizing about history, but even here they are commonly employed not as explanations in themselves, but as devices which prompt new lines of enquiry, or, as Collingwood would put it, new question-and-answer complexes. To be sure, a generalization is one of the weapons in the historian's armoury, but, unlike inference, it can never, in Collingwood's view, play a fundamental role. Unlike generalizations and laws which can form the basis of weak or strong predictions, the concern of historical explanation is solely with the past. Overall, we may reasonably conclude that by contrast with the role of generalization in science and also in ordinary language, in history, as Collingwood understands it, it is the particular that rules.

Not all of Collingwood's early readers were antipathetic to his separation of history from science. Peter Winch in his *The Idea of a Social Science* (1958) takes a line of argument in explicit support of Collingwood which resists any accommodation between scientific and historical explanations. It belongs to our concept of human conduct that it is not governed by laws. We go wrong, therefore, if we interpret motives and intentions as causes, and we lose the sense in which actions are embedded in social contexts if we look for explanations that are external to the action concerned. Winch, however, is less impressed by what he takes to be Collingwood's over-intellectual view of history. Like a number of Collingwood's early critics Winch tended to assume that the doctrine that all history is the history of thought confined history. And yet, as we have seen, for Collingwood the history of thought is not equivalent to the history of ideas. Collingwood took the view that 'historicity, too, is a matter of degree' (IH 227), but it does not follow that as thought advances in complexity history must lose interest in the everyday. Historical thinking enables us to reconstruct an ancient script or the first computer, unravel a tortuous diplomatic intrigue or an empire in decline, but, as Collingwood remarks, 'it is in the same way that we discover the thought of a friend who writes us a letter, or a stranger who crosses the street' (IH 219).

Collingwood's thought that generalization, even if true (IH 223), tells us little about what gives history its autonomy is significant, for if history is an empirical science then the capacity to construct true generalizations would be a reasonable test of its powers. History's integrity, however, lies not in observation and experiment, but in imagination and inference. A statement which aims to give an account of one event by connecting it with others must to some degree depend on imagination and inference, but on its own it can never be an explanation of them. Erase true generalizations and we lose useful historical information, but erase imagination and inference and we lose what makes historical understanding possible at all. This, surely, is Collingwood's great discovery. History is not simply defined by its subject matter; it is defined by our capacity to imagine the past and to infer its character from the evidence available. It is in this sense that historical knowledge is self-knowledge. But this means also, as Collingwood certainly wants us to see, that historical knowledge is at one and the same time present knowledge.

We can now see why generalization is in Collingwood's way of thinking peripheral to what makes history tick. The validity of a generalization is tested quite independently (and is usually prized for being so) of the attitudes of the investigator. But, if Collingwood is right, history has one perspective which it cannot shed – the present. By placing the historian at the centre of the stage Collingwood has successfully distanced history from science (and, hence, from the laws and law-like generalizations which science produces), but in doing so he encounters a problem which his first readers were quick to notice. If all history is present history how can the historian avoid present prejudice?

The problem of the relation between history and value is central to any philosophy of history, and his early reviewers commented on *The Idea of History* with this very much in mind. One was the American philosopher Arthur E. Murphy who in 1947 expressed his concern that Collingwood's otherwise admirable stress on the necessity of a perspective in historical writing understated the extent to which historical perspectives can themselves be criticized and judged (Arthur E. Murphy. (1963), 'Collingwood's Idea of History', in W. H. Hay and M. G. Singer (eds) *Reason and the Common Good, Selected Essays of Arthur E Murphy*, Englewood Cliffs, NJ: Prentice Hall, ch. 10, 125; originally published in *The Philosophical Review*, LVI, 1947, 587–92). Here we need to proceed with care. Historians assuredly write about the past from their own perspective, but without the ability to keep present concerns in perspective their histories would collapse into self-centredness and provincialism. So Collingwood has a problem; in fact he has two problems, both of which arise from his insistence that unless the historian '*has* a point of view he can see nothing at all' (IH 108). As Collingwood understands it, the historian's point of view is, first, the present because the past cannot be known at all except from the perspective of the present, and, second, the individual cluster of beliefs on the basis of which each historian judges the past to be what it is.

Since the second problem raises the question of impartiality in history and so is likely to be more familiar, we will examine it first. Here we need to step outside *The Idea of History* to ascertain Collingwood's views. In a paper entitled 'Can Historians Be Impartial?' (PH 209–19) which was delivered in January 1936 during the period of the 1930s in which much of *The Idea of History* was written, Collingwood says, surely rightly, that we would normally understand impartiality as the absence of prejudice. Historians go wrong, therefore, when they prejudge the issues before them or settle them in advance of the evidence. All historians seek to understand the past by questioning the evidence and so reaching answers that can be justified. Prejudice is finding the answer you want rather than the answer the evidence permits. However, as Collingwood concludes, the difficulty is that prejudice not only adds zest to historical curiosity; it is also the personal signature of many of the greatest historians. Moreover, to take neutrality as a value overriding all others is to set the experience of the historian aside. Since Collingwood argues that without experience re-enactment is impossible it seems that he must choose between partiality with history and impartiality without it. In fact, his solution is to separate history from chronology – the listing of dates is secure against bias, but is scarcely history – and to ask historians proper to be honestly aware of their own partisanship. Thus Collingwood states that 'without judgments of value, there is no history' (PH 217).

Here Collingwood's view is deliberately provocative because it makes the past as much dependent upon the historian's own beliefs as upon the methods and techniques used to uncover it. And, yet, Collingwood is determined to stick to his guns. Any past activity will remain elusive to the historian who is ignorant of that activity's standards and practices. Thus, historians of poetry must know what good poetry is, military historians would be unable to grasp the achievement of a Napoleon without an independent

understanding of military tactics, political historians would fail
to see the originality of a Caesar and, hence, the motives for
assassinating him, without a knowledge of political skills and
abilities. Clearly, what constitutes poetic excellence, military genius
and political intelligence involves judgements of value. Moreover,
Collingwood asserts, such judgements are necessary to history
because they provide historians with the criteria of selection they
need. Without them history would be rudderless. Thus, estimation
of the significance of historical events is a proof not of partiality,
but of engagement with history as Collingwood understands it.
History proper absolutely requires the historian to select from, for
example, the welter of assassinations in the Roman world, Caesar's
as the one that is most revealing of insight or error. As Collingwood
insists at the conclusion of his 1936 paper (PH 218), for historians
proper, judging the events they narrate as courageous, foolish or
whatever fits the bill is exactly what the re-enactment of the past
demands.

One reason for Collingwood's unwillingness to deny historians
their commitments is his firm belief in the connection between
history and life (A, chs VIII and XIX). However, Collingwood
visualizes historians going into battle as judges rather than as
advocates since he asks each specifically to be on their guard
against their own prejudices by accepting that when the evidence
runs contrary to them it is their wishes that must be set aside.

We must surely accept that the line Collingwood defends
between judgement and narrative in history is on his own terms a
narrow one. Even so it is a boundary that makes sense. Historians
may well on occasion write more like advocates than judges, but it
is possible to state the difference. Bias can be apparent and when
it is apparent it can be corrected. Biased judges or cricket umpires
reveal their prejudices in the decisions they make in the court room
or on the playing field. Although not quite in the same way, the
committed historian writing history in the spirit of his religious
or political beliefs does so from principled choice, and his works
are open to criticism and modification in the light of evidence
which may have been neglected or misinterpreted. However, when
Collingwood says the historian's perspective is that of the present
we are confronted not by a point of view which can be modified
or corrected, but by a temporal state of affairs which is necessarily
the case. All history is contemporary history, Collingwood tells us,

so confirming that the historian's perspective is neither god-like nor subjective. All history is written from the standpoint of a particular present. Medieval historians writing about the ancient world do so from their point in time. Renaissance historians writing about the medieval world do so from their present, as modern historians also do when writing about the Renaissance. There is, then, no sense in Collingwood of the historical present claiming sovereignty over the past. The claim that all history is contemporary history does not make history imperialistic. Quite the contrary, in fact, since each generation of historians will re-enact their past according to their own criteria and methodology.

In his review of *The Idea of History* Arthur Murphy expresses the view that Collingwood's doctrine that history always begins and ends in the present risks making the present more monolithic than it need be. No present is wholly lacking in diversity and divergence of view. To be sure, but this is not the real difficulty. Collingwood thinks of history as 'one of the necessary and transcendental modes of mind's activity' (IH 422); it is hardwired into the ways we think and so there is, as Collingwood puts it, 'no difference in principle, only a difference in degree, between the historical thinking done by a bricklayer in the exercise of his craft and that done by a Gibbon or a Grote' (IH 422). All historical understanding stems from the perspective of the present. Whether it is a purely practical task or an attempt to uncover the way of life of the ancient Assyrians, both must be formulated in terms of present techniques and understandings. The present, therefore, as the load-bearing concept in Collingwood's philosophy of history, is not simply a moment in time, but, in Collingwood's view, the only moment in time which we can sensibly think of as actual. Past and future are moments in time but they are ideal states; neither exists: the past because it no longer exists and the future because its existence is yet to be. Moreover, the present gives the past a permanence which it cannot give the future. For the past, the present is the only refuge. The present is the only possible medium of the past's existence. Without the present there would be no temporal dimension in which the past can be recovered, and, hence, no residue in the form of evidence for historians to reflect upon. Collingwood's point is not just that each generation of historians writes history from the perspective of its own time or that the past is relative to the age which writes about it (IH 108); it is rather, and much more importantly, that the present is the locus of history, the only region in which the past can survive and the only position from which it can be reconstructed.

Collingwood's early critics may be forgiven for thinking that history is about the past, not the present, and that if Collingwood's doctrine led to the two states being confused then it should be set aside. But, as many writers on Collingwood's philosophy of history have indicated, his point is to do with the possibility of history and not with its practice. For William H. Dray, even if we grant that history begins in the present, 'that doesn't make the subject-matter of history the present *rather than* the past' (Dray, 1995, 287). Moreover, Collingwood's understanding of historical evidence provides him with further protection. Evidence is necessarily evidence of something. Thus, the footprint in the flower border outside the study window is evidence – that the gardener or the window cleaner has been at work or that the burglar the police are investigating gained entry to the house from that direction, or that the boys from the neighbouring house have been trying to retrieve a lost ball. All of these possibilities belong in the past, but none are denied by the evidence belonging in the present. In addition, when historians disagree over what is to count as evidence or whether the absence of evidence confirms the absence of an event it is the same understanding of evidence which is hard at work. Collingwood's doctrine of the historical imagination plays a similar role. Whatever difficulties face historians in imagining what it must have been like to think in the ways of 'an Attila, a Montezuma II or an Iroquois chief' (M. C. D'Arcy. (1959), *The Sense of History, Secular and Sacred*, London: Faber, 30), they are not multiplied by the fact of the historian's present perspective. They may be multiplied by the historian's lack of imagination or by paucity and ambiguity of evidence, or by the sheer impenetrability of an alien culture, but the present is a given. Without it history would be impossible. That is surely Collingwood's basic point.

Nevertheless, it would be a mistake to think that Collingwood's position is free from criticism. The past, Collingwood assures us, can be reached only from the standpoint of the present. Historians are anything but antiquaries. On the contrary, they are rooted in their times. It is in their time that evidence is brought to life. It is in their time that the past is re-enacted. But exactly what in the present does the past stand relative to? If it is present evidence, the historical imagination and the historian's capacity to re-enact past thought, then Collingwood's position is defensible. But if it is the past relative to current problems – for example, a history of wars of intervention written from the standpoint of present theories and attitudes – then the result is surely to narrow history because the past may well have not thought about intervention in that way. If it is the past relative to current interests, then Collingwood's argument becomes more difficult to uphold. However, Collingwood can be reasonably confident that the past is grasped relative to contemporary historical methods. Since techniques of inquiry vary, often gaining in subtlety, especially in archaeology, the past does not stand still, but reaches greater permanency as inquiries become more precise. And, yet, even here, the past's independence from the present is worth re-stating because the past, when present, did not need such methods to explain itself. As Peter Winch pointed out in 1958, the medieval knight did not need to rethink his ideas of chivalry to understand them, he simply thought in those terms (Peter Winch. (1958), *The Idea of a Social Science*, London: Routledge & Kegan Paul, 132).

Collingwood often speaks of history as educating the present on how it has come to be what it is. All history is contemporary history, then, in the sense that the past is not remote from the present, but directly antecedent to it. This is what Collingwood means when he speaks about the connection between history and self-knowledge. But surely, Collingwood's critics will argue, this not only limits history to the routes which have led to the present, (much in the past may be thought of as wholly unrelated to the historian's present; the past when present is not a road to anywhere), it does so on the parochial assumption that the present is what the past is leading up to. And, yet, critics should tread carefully, for Collingwood explicitly warns against the claim that the present can embrace the past in its entirety. He writes: 'the perceptible-here-and-now can never be perceived, still less interpreted in its entirety; and the infinite process of past time can never be envisaged as a whole' (IH 247). With this as its governing ideal, history must end in failure. To come alive the historian's thought must spring from an act of sympathy with its object. Collingwood writes: 'every new generation must re-write history in its own way' (IH 248).

In his review of *The Idea of History* in 1952 Leo Strauss draws out the implications of Collingwood's view (Leo Strauss. (1952), 'On Collingwood's Philosophy of History', *The Review of Metaphysics*, 5, 4, 559–86). If all of history stems from the present and if each present writes history anew, then any impartial estimation of the significance of historical events would seem to be impossible. Given Collingwood's aversion to the attempt to discover patterns in the historical process, we can easily see why his early critics had a point. As the past can be grasped only from the point of view of the present, history is both retrospective and necessarily open to correction. So when Collingwood claims that 'the historian can genuinely see into the past only so far as he stands firmly rooted in the present' (IH 60), this must be thought of as a paradox, perhaps even a contradiction. And, yet, this is a feature of history that Collingwood takes extremely seriously. A present perspective is constitutive of all historical writing. It is not a limit to understanding the past, or an obstacle that we might sensibly imagine being removed or modified in some way.

As early reviewers like Strauss were fully aware, Collingwood's position not only raises substantial difficulties on its own account; it also seems to fly in the face of a number of his central doctrines. Historical understanding, as Collingwood pictures it, proceeds by re-enactment. The past is to be re-enacted on its terms. Past thoughts, purposes, policies, the questions to which past agents sought answers in their actions – all of these are primary. What the historian re-enacts is the past seen as a separate world, one whose self-understandings are its bedrock and, hence, the focus of all historical investigation. But the insistence that the past can be grasped only from the vantage point of the present changes everything. For the historian knows how past events unfolded. The historian knows the consequences of past purposes and policies where those who lived at the time did not. The gift that a present perspective gives to history is the gift of hindsight which means, as Leo Strauss realizes (Strauss, 1952, 575), that from the perspective of the present the historian must be a spectator of the past. Since the historian knows how events have panned out – the consequences of the treaty, the changes the invention made to the way of life – any re-enactment of the past is never solely on the past's terms. Certainly, without the re-enactment of an agent's thoughts historical understanding would be impossible, but it would be equally impossible without the perspective of the present, one which embraces more than the past was able to know.

It is true that ideas are seminal or battles decisive only in retrospect, but it is also the case that there must come a point when any unfolding of events ceases. Even so, Collingwood's insight that the present is the key to the past remains, and it is noticed by Strauss as not only central to what makes *The Idea of History* distinctive, but also contentious for lying behind Collingwood's view that historical knowledge is relative to a present perspective on the past is the belief that each present is 'the highest point that has ever existed' (Strauss, 1952, 561). Or, as Collingwood himself puts it, 'the present is always perfect in the sense that it always succeeds in being what it is trying to be' (IH 109). Not that present societies or historical periods are ever entirely consistent with themselves, a point that Collingwood uses to confer on historians the role of distinguishing 'between retrograde and progressive elements' (IH 135) in the age they are studying. As Strauss points out (Strauss, 1952, 562), Collingwood's own methodology in examining the history of the philosophy of history in Parts I to IV of *The Idea of History* is a perfect illustration of this dictum because it selects its material in accordance with the notion of 'scientific' history that Collingwood in his present wishes to defend. In being relative to the present as opposed to the past or the future, historical knowledge is relative to the only vantage point which is open to it. The past may be viewed in no other way. Thus, for Collingwood, 'the historian's problem is a present problem, not a future one: it is to interpret the material now available, not to anticipate future discoveries' (IH 180). For Strauss, this means that Collingwood's philosophy of history is torn between reason and romanticism, and so he writes of Collingwood,

> he vacillated between two different views of history, the rationalistic view of Hegel and the non-rationalistic view. He never clearly realized that these two views are mutually incompatible. The historical reason for this failure was his lack of acquaintance with Nietzsche's epoch-making critique of 'scientific history.'
> (Strauss, 1952, 563)

Reactions

Historical relativism is the topic which dominates in the early discussion of *The Idea of History*. Indeed, for some critics,

Collingwood's aim was not only to defend a specific account of historical knowledge, but also to show why on this account philosophy can have no existence independent of history. In his review, Strauss interprets Collingwood as calling for 'the fusion of philosophy and history' (Strauss, 1952, 563) and in a review published in 1947 Michael Oakeshott, a philosopher who was as keen as Collingwood to defend history against the prevailing dogmas of positivism, expressed similar concerns. After praising Collingwood's skills as an historian of ideas and noting his linkage of history with self-knowledge, Oakeshott commented, 'it must be observed that, almost imperceptibly, Collingwood's philosophy of history turned into a philosophy in which all knowledge is assimilated to historical knowledge, and consequently into a radically sceptical philosophy' (Michael Oakeshott. (1947), *The English Historical Review*, LXII, 84–6, 85).

There is no doubt that early readings of *The Idea of History* were shaped by T.M. Knox's Introduction and, hence, by his view that Collingwood's later thought moved towards historicism. Modern readers, by contrast, have the considerable advantages of, first, the revised edition of *The Idea of History* together with the Lectures on History of 1926 to 1928 (1993); second, *The Principles of History* (1999) which reprints almost everything of significance that Collingwood wrote on history; third, the editor's introductions to both of these works which set them in their appropriate context and provide a detailed examination of the manuscripts, including textual differences and discrepancies; fourth, Collingwood's essays in the philosophy of history, usefully collected in Debbins (1965); and fifth, a rich body of secondary literature on Collingwood's philosophy of history and the issues which arise from it including those of relativism and scepticism.

It is valuable when reading *The Idea of History* to take note of a double distinction. There is, first, the difference between the development of Collingwood's thought and its place in our own. It is, of course, important to be clear about what exactly Collingwood is saying on any given topic, but intellectual biography and philosophy are separate activities. Finding out what Collingwood said about history when and why he said it (or said little or nothing at all) is not the same as arguing with him. Second, it is necessary to distinguish between the arguments themselves. Questions concerning the relativity of history have a bearing upon questions concerning the relation between history and philosophy, but the issues these raise are different. A characteristic feature of Collingwood as a philosopher is his determination to seek out avoidable dualisms. One dualism arises when history and philosophy are falsely understood. Thus when history is conceived as the study of past facts established as such by the authorities who vouch for them, then critical history, 'scientific' history as Collingwood understands it, is blocked, and any accommodation with philosophy made impossible. Similarly, if philosophy is conceived of as a court to which history is subject, then it is history which suffers through, for example, inappropriate comparison with natural science or by forced identification with a single idea (IH 492). In other words, what Collingwood seeks is not the identification of philosophy and history, but, to use his own term (A 77), a 'rapprochement' between them. The quarrel between history and philosophy can be avoided only if both are properly understood. Historical relativism now appears in a new and potentially troubling light. For if Collingwood is an historical relativist then relativism is what critical history, history proper as Collingwood describes it, must involve. And this means that any accommodation of philosophy with history comes at a price.

We should first be clear about the nature of Collingwood's relativism. In what sense is Collingwood's account of history proper relativistic? If by historical relativism is meant, as W.H. Dray puts it (see Dray, 1995, ch. 8), 'the doctrine that what historians assert must always be understood as expressing a judgment relative to the person making it' (Dray, 1995, 271), then we surely have to conclude that Collingwood is an historical relativist. Further, if we can add to this the doctrine that what historians assert is always relative to their present perspective, then we must surely reach the same conclusion. Collingwood's comment that what historians think of 'the achievements of the Middle Ages will necessarily differ according as the historian is a man of the eighteenth, nineteenth, or twentieth century' (IH 108) brings the point home. Little of importance follows from this, however, since we can be equally sure that Collingwood does not believe that historians construct their accounts of the past at will, nor if Collingwood is right about history proper should we ourselves believe that when an historian expresses an opinion on a given historical topic – say, the complicity of officials in Vichy regarding the Nazi treatment of French Jews

– or a given historical period – say, general British attitudes during the abdication crisis in the 1930s – that there is nothing more that can be said by way of evaluation and criticism. Collingwood, we might say, may be counted an historical relativist, but not a sceptic, and the reason for this is clear. Knowledge of the past is not like knowledge derived from observation or experiment. It is not like memory. Nor does it derive from the statements of authorities. Nor, as Collingwood was at pains to tell generations of students in his lectures, is it knowledge of the past in its completeness ('history is an illusion, if it means knowledge of the past in its actuality and completeness' IH 484). No historian treats each historical fact with equal importance; as Collingwood remarks, 'the name of the hundredth man to be put out of action by musketry fire' (IH 484) is unimportant to the historian of the Battle of Waterloo unless it is relevant in some way to the questions he wishes to ask. Here is the key to Collingwood's understanding of certainty in history and the reason for his rejection of scepticism. Certainty in history stems from the evidence and the historian's interrogation of it. Thus, in an introductory lecture to a course on the philosophy of history which was unavailable to his early reviewers, but is available to us and must surely have been common knowledge among the students who attended, we find Collingwood arguing that 'the certainty of history, then, is the certainty that the evidence in our possession points to one particular answer to the question we ask of it' (IH 487). There is certainty in history, but it is a certainty which is linked, first, to the special character of the past as Collingwood understands it, second, to the presence of evidence, and third, to Collingwood's own logic of question and answer. In other words, it is not that the absence of evidence would make our knowledge of the past uncertain. Without evidence there would be no past to question, and without questions historical knowledge would not be possible at all.

   The second worry which concerns Strauss and Oakeshott in their reviews is that Collingwood's historical relativism ends in the collapse of philosophy into history. In order to assess this we need to follow a more complicated route. Here the prime requirement is for readers to trust Collingwood's own description of his aims. Once it is seen that the purpose underlying Collingwood's philosophy of history is not the identification of philosophy with history, but their 'rapprochement' (A 77), then the different ways in which this is elaborated should become transparent.

'Rapprochement' asks Collingwood to reveal the similarities and differences between history and philosophy, together with the ways in which they are related. Philosophy is distinguished in terms of its aims and methods. It is self-reflective where history is not and its search for the criteria which govern understandings in art, religion, science and history itself is one that is beyond their individual remits. And, yet, the distinctiveness of philosophy does not mean that it is lacking a close connection with history. Quite the contrary, in fact, because at the close of his 1928 Lectures on the Philosophy of History Collingwood explained their mutual dependence in the following way: 'History supplies philosophy with data, and philosophy supplies history with methods' (IH 496). Where the philosophy of history is concerned the interaction is both tighter and, Collingwood believes, more significant. Thus, in the Introduction to *The Idea of History* (perhaps the key to the whole book), Collingwood spells out what he means by a philosophy of history and why it is important. Here we encounter for the first time Collingwood's remarkable claim that to the modern intellect philosophy and history bear a particular and puzzling relationship: 'Particular' because Collingwood understands the history of philosophy as the history of philosophical problems. Just as in the Greek world the central problem for philosophy to solve was its relation to mathematics and in the medieval world its relation to theology and in the post-seventeenth-century European world its relation to science, so, Collingwood argues, in the modern world, Collingwood's own world, philosophy's focus comes from history – its nature, methods and procedures. 'Puzzling' because traditional epistemology totally fails to account for the kind of knowledge historical knowledge is and what makes it possible. This is the puzzle that realism is unable to solve. Thus, any philosophy that approaches history by the methods which work for science is bound to disappoint. It is in this sense that Collingwood defends 'a general overhauling of all philosophical questions in the light of the results reached by the philosophy of history' (IH 6–7).

Elaborations of the interconnection between philosophy and history follow. Thus, philosophers exploring the character of historical enquiry are encouraged not to ignore what historians actually do. Moreover, the more skilled the historian, in Collingwood's view, the more philosophers can learn. Collingwood advises philosophers to turn to historians whose experience of

historical work is 'better grounded than a man's opinions of
the French people based on a single week-end visit to Paris'
(IH 7). Further, as Collingwood makes abundantly clear in *An
Autobiography*, (A, chs VII–IX), philosophy's relation with its
own history will be transformed once the implications of his new
theory of history are understood. By placing philosophical ideas in
their historical context many fallacies can be avoided and, to use
Collingwood's own terminology, the right questions asked.

Collingwood's early reviewers were well aware that the best
context for understanding his thought generally is the tradition of
idealist liberalism which forms the background to much of what
he says. Synthesis between philosophy and history is also a major
neo-Hegelian concern, but even though Collingwood devotes a
great deal of effort to arguing about this topic with, for example, the
Italian idealist philosopher Croce (IH 190–204), the concepts which
inform his view of history are his own. Croce was no archaeologist,
and Collingwood derives much in the form of practical experience
and intellectual stimulus from his extensive and detailed archaeological work on Roman Britain. Archaeology forms at least part of
the origin and most of the testing ground for the logic of question
and answer, historical evidence and inference, notions which make
up the core of Collingwood's philosophy of history. And, yet, there
are problems that archaeological investigation alone is unable
to solve. Thus, Collingwood explicitly grounds his revolution in
history in a combination of 'the empirical methodology of archaeological science and the pure methodology of philosophy' (IH 427).
By such means, Collingwood argues, the historian will be able

> not indeed to 'know' the past as it actually happened, which
> he neither can do nor wants to do, but to solve with accuracy
> and certainty the particular historical problems which present
> themselves to his mind, in terms of the evidence at his disposal.
> (IH 427)

Influences and affinities

It was Collingwood's firm belief that the philosophy of history is
not a minor subdivision of philosophy, but essential to its structure

and character. If philosophy is self-reflective, then it must have an intimate connection with history. It was the failure of analytical philosophy to recognize this that largely provoked Collingwood's attacks on it (A 35, 47, 51–2). Even so, the limits of history as Collingwood identifies them can be as enlightening as its strengths. History can have no concern with the future. How, then, are we to estimate the impact of a past philosopher's ideas except from our own present point of view? We read Collingwood in the light of what is important to us, as he himself read Bradley, Croce and the other philosophers with whom he argues. The future of Collingwood's revolution in history clearly mattered to him. *The Idea of History* teaches the value of history to all generations, not just to Collingwood's own.

When we realize the extent of Collingwood's ambitions for history it is hard not to conclude that, to some degree unavoidably, *The Idea of History* as it was published in 1946 let him down. Like all true revolutionaries Collingwood wanted to ensure that there was no going back. Thinking about history on the model of natural science must be overthrown and a new way of understanding put in its place. However, while this negative purpose is compelling and largely achieved, the proposed replacement is less so. In part (and this must be seen as a substantial part), this is because Collingwood's philosophy of history remained uncompleted. Whereas *The Principles of Art* (1938) tells us pretty much all we need to know about Collingwood's aesthetics and *The New Leviathan* (1942), hurried and impatiently written though much of it often is, about politics, *The Idea of History* of 1946 does not tell us all we need to know about his views on history. Much of importance, such as the logic of question and answer, is discussed elsewhere (A, ch. V). More significantly, the revolution to embrace the new principles of history did not take place as planned with many of its central ideas left unconnected and some, such as the doctrine of encapsulation, not fully worked out.

With this in mind, the status of *The Idea of History* as one of the iconic texts of twentieth-century philosophy needs further explanation. To remedy the defects in analytical philosophy a number of mid-to late twentieth-century historians and philosophers turned their attention to continental philosophy only to find that Collingwood had already made that journey himself.

Historians of ideas, such as Quentin Skinner, soon saw that it was impossible to clarify what they wanted to say about the history of political thought without taking Collingwood's advances into account. For Collingwood taught that the history of ideas did not consist in different answers to the same question, but in different questions, the logical structure of which it was the historian's job to reconstruct. It was not that philosophical issues had become historical (although to some at the time it must have seemed that way), but rather that the historical sense itself had been refreshed, so facilitating a clearer understanding of what political philosophers in different historical periods were about.

One reason for Collingwood's work having a permanent claim on us lies in its account of how an influential past is possible at all. Thus, Collingwood's insights into the importance of history have been felt in contemporary moral philosophy, especially in the challenges to modernity laid down by Alasdair MacIntyre (1981) in his *After Virtue* (London: Duckworth). So when MacIntyre, as a contemporary moral philosopher, explicitly acknowledges his debt to Collingwood, he is able to repay it in currency which is not Collingwood's own. MacIntyre's condemnation of modernity and his reconstruction of virtue in the modern context both exploit Collingwood's revolution in history, but they do so in terms which Collingwood would find hard to recognize. MacIntyre makes his debt to Collingwood absolutely plain. He insists, like Collingwood, that any history, including that of the modern world which MacIntyre considered fallen, cannot be neutral, but must presuppose standards. He writes, 'It is what Hegel called philosophical history and what Collingwood took all successful historical writing to be' (MacIntyre, 1981, 3). In a similar fashion, Collingwood's insight that historical statements do not operate like propositional statements is built on by Hans-Georg Gadamer in his *Truth and Method* (English translation 1975) in terms which are emphatically his own. Here, Collingwood's view of history is extended to embrace current concerns. Learning from the past, then, involves developing the past in circumstances which are unfamiliar, possibly strange to it. The philosophy of history after Collingwood is not the philosophy of history as it was for him or as it was for those by whom he was influenced.

Conclusion

Collingwood wanted history to have an educational value. History requires us to understand the past on its own terms. It involves reconstructing a way of life in its own particular context. But Collingwood also teaches that no reconstruction of the past is possible except from the perspective of the present. Thus, the past is not wholly remote from the present but lives on in it. Learning from an alien, possibly primitive culture can take place even though the features of its way of life from which we learn are absent from our own, but if the past did not exist in the present in the form of evidence we could not understand it at all.

The significance of *The Idea of History* is that it teaches us how to think about history in non-realist terms. Collingwood's philosophy of history is penetrated with arguments derived from his philosophy of mind and of action, which means that its main principles – that all history is the history of thought and that all history is contemporary history – are both heavily indebted to his wider philosophical views. In arriving at these basic positions the aim was not to lecture historians on how to go about their work, but rather to show how history is possible. Even so, Collingwood did believe that the historian's 'business is not to leap clean out of his own period of history but to be in every respect a man of his age and to see the past as it appears from the standpoint of that age' (IH 60). That, of course, is what Collingwood himself was, and so his own philosophy of history reflects on the problems of his age as he as a philosopher and historian conceived of them. Collingwood's revolution in history takes place against a background of conflict between religion and science with historical knowledge as the prize. His achievement is to show us clearly that history belongs to neither. History does not exhibit God's pattern for the world, nor can it be grasped by the methods of natural science. History is autonomous. Collingwood knew very well that his revolution had predecessors. It arose in a context in which much work to retrieve and develop the historical habit of mind had already been done. In this sense, the first part of *The Idea of History* is a repaying of debts, since it traces the thinking about history which led up to Collingwood's own. But Collingwood did a lot more than merely build on the ideas of others. For the revolution instituted by

Collingwood's text is found in the concepts he uses to tell us what history is, and these are new. Hegel's *Lectures on the History of Philosophy* is praised by Collingwood as 'a triumph of historical method' (IH 120), since it shows us why the history of philosophy is not 'the decanting of ready-made thoughts out of one mind into another' (IH 313). Collingwood sees philosophy and its history as mutually engaged. The aim is to show how the solutions to one set of problems give rise to new and different problems, and how these in turn create the environment for the thought of their successors. Nor are such problems solely intellectual. History embraces what we think and what we do. Here Collingwood's liberalism touches a contemporary nerve. The echo of Hegel is unmistakable, but the concepts which Collingwood uses to drive his revolution forward are entirely his own. Moreover, Collingwood's innovations embody the radical character of historical re-enactment as he understands it. Passengers on Collingwood Lines will go nowhere if they sit listening passively to their guide. Each generation reflects on history in terms of its own problems and in its own voice. Readers of *The Idea of History* soon discover that, for them, neither history nor philosophy will ever be the same.

GLOSSARY:

Collingwood's main terminology of history in his own words

Incapsulation

So long as the past and present are outside one another, knowledge of the past is not of much use in the problems of the present. But suppose the past lives on in the present; suppose though incapsulated in it, and at first sight hidden beneath the present's contradictory and more prominent features, it is still alive and active; then the historian may very well be related to the non-historian as the trained woodsman is to the ignorant traveller.

(A 100)

Inside/outside

The historian, investigating any event in the past, makes a distinction between what may be called the outside and the inside of an event. By the outside of an event I mean everything belonging to it which can be described in terms of bodies and their movements. ... By the inside of an event I mean that in it which can only be described in terms of thought.

(IH 213)

Question and answer

Question and evidence in history are correlative. Anything is evidence which enables you to answer your question – the question you are asking now.

(IH 281)

Re-enactment

The historian not only re-enacts past thought, he re-enacts it in the context of his own knowledge and therefore, in re-enacting it, criticizes it, forms his own judgement of its value, corrects whatever errors he can discern in it.

(IH 215)

Scissors and paste

Scissors-and-paste historians study periods; they collect all the extant testimony about a certain limited group of events, and hope in vain that something will come of it. Scientific historians study problems; they ask questions, and if they are good historians they ask questions which they see their way to answering.

(IH 281)

FURTHER READING

1 Background to the text

The key texts for further reading in each section of this chapter appear as follows.

Text

R. G. Collingwood. (1946), *The Idea of History*, with an Editor's Preface by T. M. Knox, Oxford: Clarendon Press; R. G. Collingwood. (1993), *The Idea of History*, Revised Edition, edited with an introduction by Jan van der Dussen, Clarendon Press, Oxford: Oxford University Press (paperback 1994). The 1993 edition reprints the 1946 text in its entirety, but leaves out Knox's original Preface. It also includes a number of previously unpublished manuscripts, including The Idea of a Philosophy of something and, in particular, a Philosophy of History (1927), Lectures on the Philosophy of History (1926) and Outlines of a Philosophy of History (1928). (All references to *The Idea of History* are to this edition.) For textual matters concerning *The Idea of History*, including the history of T. M. Knox's involvement in it and the associated problems that resulted, Knox's original Preface together with Jan van der Dussen's Introduction are both essential reading. A useful collection of Collingwood's writings on history is William Debbins. (1965), *R. G. Collingwood, Essays in the Philosophy of History*, Austin: University of Texas Press. For Collingwood's letters, including those to Clarendon Press, see Peter Johnson. (1998), *The Correspondence of R. G. Collingwood, An Illustrated Guide*, Swansea: The R. G. Collingwood Society. For the background to the *Principles of History*, textual history, discussion of contents, the text itself and detailed bibliography, including much about its significance, see R. G. Collingwood, (1999), *The Principles of History and other Writings in Philosophy of History*, edited with an Introduction by W. H. Dray and W. J. van der Dussen, Oxford: Oxford University Press. Helpful in understanding the background to the *Principles of History* are the following: W. H. Dray. (1997), 'Broadening the Historian's Subject-matter in The Principles of History', *Collingwood Studies*, IV, 2–33; David Boucher. (1997), 'The Significance of R. G. Collingwood's Principles of History', *Journal of the History of Ideas*, 58, 309–30, and also his (1995), 'The Principles of History and the Cosmology Conclusion to The Idea of Nature', *Collingwood Studies*, II, 140–70, and Jan van der Dussen. (1997), 'Collingwood's "Lost" Manuscript of The Principles of History', *History and Theory*, 36, 32–62. Since 1978 Collingwood's manuscripts have been located in the Bodleian Library, Oxford; for discussion of them see W. J. van der Dussen. (1979), 'Collingwood's Unpublished Manuscripts', *History and Theory*, 18, 287–315; and for a listing see the *Catalogue of the Papers of R. G. Collingwood (1889–1943) (Dep. Collingwood 1–28)*, compiled by Ruth A. Burchnall, Bodleian Library, Oxford, 1994 (for philosophy of history and historiography, see *Dep. Collingwood 4–7*). There are also useful listings in Donald S. Taylor. (1988), *R. G. Collingwood A Bibliography*, New York and London: Garland Publishing, and Christopher Dreisbach. (1993), *R. G. Collingwood, A Bibliographic Checklist*, Bowling Green, OH: The Philosophy Documentation Centre, Bowling Green State University.

Context

Helpful to understanding the origins of *The Idea of History* is Douglas H. Johnson. (1994), 'W. G. Collingwood and the Beginnings of *The Idea of History*', *Collingwood Studies*, I, 1–26; also useful is James Lund. (1999), 'The Idea of the History of Philosophy: Beginnings', *Collingwood Studies*, V, 1–27. On the historical context to Collingwood's *The Idea of History* the following books are important – William H. Dray. (1995), *History as Re-enactment, R. G. Collingwood's Idea of History*, Oxford: Clarendon Press, esp. chs 1 and 5 (Dray's work is a substantial and wide-ranging discussion which covers the whole of Collingwood's philosophy of history including *The Idea of History* and should be considered essential reading); W. J. van der Dussen. (1981), *History as a Science, the Philosophy of R. G. Collingwood*, The Hague: Martinus Nijhoff should also be considered essential reading. It is a major study of the nature, origins and development of Collingwood's philosophy of history, including *The Idea of History*, as well as other published and unpublished writings, including lectures. It contains an extensive bibliography of primary and secondary material and should be considered a fundamental source.

For general background in English philosophical thinking about history see Christopher Parker. (2000), *The English Idea of History*, Aldershot: Ashgate.

Collingwood and Vico

For Collingwood's views on Vico see IH Part II 7i; also important are R. G. Collingwood. (1930), *The Philosophy of History*, London: The Historical Association, Bell and Co., reprinted in Debbins, 121–39, and Collingwood's own translation of Benedetto Croce. (1913), *The Philosophy of Giambattista Vico*, London: Howard Latimer; for discussion of Collingwood's views, see Nathan Rotenstreich. (1958), *Between Past and Present*, New Haven, CT: Yale University Press; Joseph M. Levine. (1980), 'Collingwood, Vico and the Autobiography', *Clio*, 9, 3, 379–92, and also his 'Collingwood and Vico', in G. Tagliacozzo, (ed.), (1981), *Vico Past and Present*, New Jersey: Atlantic Highlands, 72–84; B. A. Haddock, 'Vico and the Problem of Historical Reconstruction' and Lionel Rubinoff, 'Vico and the Verification of Historical Interpretation', both in G. Tagliacozzo *et al.*, (eds). (1976), *Giambattista Vico and Contemporary Thought*, New Jersey: Humanities Press, 123–9, and 94–121; B. A. Haddock, 'Vico, Collingwood and the Character of a Historical Philosophy', in David Boucher, James Connolly and Tariq Modood (eds). (1995), *Philosophy, History and Civilization, Interdisciplinary Perspectives on R. G. Collingwood*, Cardiff: University of Wales Press, 130–51. Also useful is Alessandra Olivetti. (1978), 'Collingwood E Vico', *Bullettino del Centro di Studi Vichiani*, 8, 115–18, and, more generally, Leon Pompa. (1990), *Human Nature and Historical Knowledge: Hume, Hegel and Vico*, Cambridge: Cambridge University Press.

Collingwood and Croce

For Collingwood's views on Croce see IH Part IV 4i–v; also important is R.G. Collingwood. (1921), 'Croce's Philosophy of History', Hibbert Journal, 19, 263–78, reprinted in Debbins, 3–22; for discussion of Collingwood's views of Croce in general and including more particularly their own views on history, see G. R. G. Mure. (1954), 'Benedetto Croce and Oxford', *Philosophical Quarterly*, 4, 327–31; Angelo A. de Gennaro. (1965), 'Croce and Collingwood', *The Personalist*, 46, 193–202; Alan Donagan. (1972), 'Collingwood's Debt to Croce', *Mind,* 81, 265–6; Antonio Musolino, (1976), 'Collingwood e Croce', *Rivista di Studi Crociani*, 13, 390–408; James Connelly. (1995), 'Art Thou the Man, Croce, Gentile or de Ruggiero?', in Boucher *et al.*, 92–114; Harold Smart. (1962), *Philosophy and Its History*, La Salle: Open Court, esp. ch. 4; Rik Peters. (1995), 'Croce, Gentile and Collingwood on the Relation between History and Philosophy', in Boucher *et al.*, 152–68. The following also contains much useful material: L. M. Palmer and H. S. Harris. (1975), *Thought, Action and Intuition, A Symposium on the Philosophy of Benedetto Croce*, Hildesheim: Olms.

Collingwood and Bradley

For Collingwood's views on Bradley see IH Part IV, Ii, ii; for discussion see F.H. Bradley. (1968), *The Presuppositions of Critical History*, edited with an Introduction and Commentary by Lionel Rubinoff, Chicago, IL: Quadrangle Books, and the more recent F. H. Bradley. (1993), *The Presuppositions of Critical History*, edited by Guy Stock, Bristol: Thoemmes Press, and Lionel Rubinoff. (1996), 'The Autonomy of History: Collingwood's Critique of F. H. Bradley's Copernican Revolution in Historical Knowledge', in James Bradley, (ed.), (1996), *Philosophy after F. H. Bradley*, Bristol: Thoemmes Press, 127–46.

Collingwood and Hegel

For Collingwood's views on Hegel see IH Part III, 7–8; for discussion see T. M. Knox. (1961), 'Hegel in the English Speaking Countries Since 1919', *Hegel-Studien*, 1, 315–8, and Gary K. Browning. (2004), *Rethinking R. G. Collingwood, Philosophy,*

Politics and the Unity of Theory and Practice, London: Palgrave Macmillan, esp. ch. 4.

Collingwood and Oakeshott

For Collingwood's views on Oakeshott see IH Part IV, I, v; also important is Collingwood's review of Oakeshott's Experience and its Modes, (1933), in *The Cambridge Review*, 16 February 1934, reprinted in Eric Homberger, William Janeway and Simon Schama (eds). (1970), *The Cambridge Mind, Ninety Years of the Cambridge Review 1879–1969*, London: Jonathan Cape, 132–4, and also in *Collingwood Studies*, IV, 1997, 188–9; for discussion see David Boucher. (1984), 'The Creation of the Past: British Idealism and Michael Oakeshott's Philosophy of History', *History and Theory*, 23, 193–214, and Boucher.(1989), 'Overlap and Autonomy: The Different Worlds of Collingwood and Oakeshott', *Storia, Antropologiae scienze del linguaggio*, IV, 2–3, 69–89, and (1993), 'Human Conduct, History and Social Science in the Works of R. G. Collingwood and Michael Oakeshott', *New Literary History*, 24, 697–717. Also useful is James Connelly. (1997), 'R. G. Collingwood and Michael Oakeshott, "Art, History and Science"', *Collingwood Studies*, IV, 184–96.

Collingwood and Toynbee

For Collingwood's views on Toynbee see IH Part IV, I, vi, for Toynbee's criticism of Collingwood's view of history see (1954), *A Study of History*, Oxford: Oxford University Press, Vol. IX, 718–37; for discussion see E. D. Myers. (1947), 'A Note on Collingwood's Criticism of Toynbee', *Journal of Philosophy*, 44, 485–9, and Hayden V. White. (1957), 'Collingwood and Toynbee: Transitions in English Historical Thought', *English Miscellany*, 9, 147–78.

Collingwood and Spengler

For Collingwood's views on Spengler see IH Part IV 2 vi; also important is R. G. Collingwood. (1927), 'Oswald Spengler and the Theory of Historical Cycles', *Antiquity*, I, 311–25, and (1927), 'The Theory of Historical Cycles', *Antiquity*, I, 435–46, reprinted in Debbins, 57–75 and 76–89.

Collingwood and Dilthey

For Collingwood's views on Dilthey see IH Part IV, 2, iv; for discussion see H. A. Hodges. (1952), *The Philosophy of Wilhelm Dilthey*, London: Routledge, esp. ch. 10, and Robert C. Scharff. (1976), 'Non-analytical Unspeculative Philosophy of History: The Legacy of Wilhelm Dilthey', *Cultural Hermeneutics*, 3, 295–331.

Development

Collingwood's own account of the development of his thought is the most important; see R. G. Collingwood. (1939), *An Autobiography*, Oxford: Clarendon Press (reprinted with an Introduction by Stephen Toulmin, Oxford: Clarendon Press, 1970). For accounts of the general development of Collingwood's thought which contain much on the development of his thought on history see David Boucher. (1995), 'The Life, Times and Legacy of R. G. Collingwood', in Boucher *et al.*, 1–31, and Fred Inglis. (2009), *History Man The Life of R. G. Collingwood*, Princeton, NJ: Princeton University Press which, as its title suggests, contains much on the importance of history to Collingwood throughout his working life.

   The unity of Collingwood's thought, including the radical conversion hypothesis, namely that his later writings display a conversion to historicism, has aroused controversy; for this see in addition to T. M. Knox's Editor's Preface to *The Idea of History* (1946) and works by van der Dussen already mentioned, Alan Donagan. (1962), *The Later Philosophy of R. G. Collingwood*, Oxford: Clarendon Press, (reprinted with a new Preface, (1985), Chicago: University of Chicago Press); Louis O. Mink. (1969), *Mind, History and Dialectic, The Philosophy of R. G. Collingwood*, Bloomington: Indiana University Press, and Lionel Rubinoff. (1970), *Collingwood and the Reform of Metaphysics, A Study in the Philosophy of Mind*, Toronto: University of Toronto Press and also his (1996), 'Collingwood and the Radical Conversion Hypothesis', *Dialogue*, 5, 1, 71–83. For a first-rate discussion of the issues involved, see James Connelly. (2003), *Metaphysics, Method and Politics, The Political Philosophy of R. G. Collingwood*, Exeter: Imprint Academic, esp. ch. 1, and also his (1990), 'Metaphysics and Method: A Necessary Unity in the Philosophy of R. G. Collingwood', *Storia Anthropologia e Scienze de Linguaggio*, 5, 1–2, Rome.

For the development of Collingwood's views on history see A. F. Wilson. (2001), 'Collingwood's Forgotten Historiographic Revolution', *Collingwood Studies*, VIII, 6–72.

Collingwood's idea of history: structural features

Louis O. Mink, 'Collingwood's Historicism: A Dialectic of Process', in Michael Krausz (ed.), (1972), *Critical Essays on the Philosophy of R.G. Collingwood*, Oxford: Clarendon Press, 154–78; Stephen Toulmin, 'Conceptual Change and the Problem of Relativity' in Krausz, 1972, 201–21; Nathan Rotenstreich, 'Metaphysics and Historicism', in Krausz, 1972, 179–200; E. Gellner, 'Thought and Time, or the Reluctant Relativist', in I. C. Jarvie and J. Agassi, (eds). (1974), *The Devil in Modern Philosophy*, London: Routledge, 151–65; T. Modood. (1989), 'The Later Collingwood's Alleged Historicism and Relativism', *Journal of the History of Philosophy*, 27, 1, 101–25; Rex Martin. (1995), 'Collingwood's Claim that Metaphysics is an Historical Discipline', Boucher *et al.*, 1995, 203–45, and Phillip Brown. (1998), 'Was Collingwood a Relativist?', *Collingwood Studies*, V, 43–71.

2 Collingwood's great discovery: the autonomy of history

The key texts for reading in each section of this chapter appear as follows.

Realism

R. G. Collingwood. (1939), *An Autobiography*, Oxford: Oxford University Press, 1939, ch. VI; IH 142, 181.

W. H. Dray. (1957), 'R. G. Collingwood and the Acquaintance Theory of Knowledge', *Revue Internationale de Philosophe*, 11, 420–32; John Frederic Post. (1965), 'Does Knowing Make a Difference to What is Known?', *Philosophical Quarterly*, 15, 220–28; Alan Donagan. (1966), 'Does Knowing Make a Difference to What is Known? A Rejoinder to Mr. Post', *Philosophical Quarterly*, 16, 35, 2–5; Alan Donagan. (1975), 'Realism and Historical Instrumentalism', *Revue Internationale de Philosophe*, 29, 78–89; Harriet Gilliam. (1976), 'The Dialectics of Realism and Idealism in Modern Historiographic Theory', *History and Theory*, 15, 231–56; Leon Pompa. (1981), 'Truth and Fact in History', in L. Pompa and W. H. Dray (eds). *Substance and Form in History, A Collection of Essays in the Philosophy of History Presented to W. H. Walsh*, Edinburgh: University of Edinburgh Press, 171–86, and M. Marion. (2000), 'Oxford Realism: Knowledge and Perception I', *British Journal for the History of Philosophy*, 8, 2, 299–338, and (2000) 'Oxford Realism: Knowledge and Perception II', *British Journal for the History of Philosophy*, 8, 3, 485–519.

History – is it art or science?

The Historical Imagination Part V, Section 3, in IH 242–3 and 249–53; for sources outside IH see R. G. Collingwood. (1923), 'History and Science', *The Vasculum*, 9, 2, 52–9 (reprinted in *Collingwood Studies*, IV, 1997, 197–205); (1922), 'Are History and Science Different Kinds of Knowledge?', *Mind*, 31, 443–51 (reprinted in Debbins, 23–33); (1924/5), 'The Nature and Aims of a Philosophy of History', *Proceedings of the Aristotelian Society*, 25, 151–74 (reprinted in Debbins, 34–56). For useful discussion see J. van der Dussen. (2007), 'Collingwood's Claim that History is a Science', *Collingwood and British Idealism Studies*, 13, 2, 5–30; James Connelly. (1997), 'Natural Science, History and Christianity', *Collingwood Studies*, IV, 101–32; Melvin Rader. (1967), 'Art and History', *Journal of Aesthetics and Art Criticism*, 26, 157–68, and Donald S. Taylor. (1973), 'R. G. Collingwood: Art, Craft and History', *Clio*, 2, 239–78.

The autonomy of history

Human Nature and Human History, Part V, Section I and *The Subject-matter of History*, Part V, Section 5 of *The Idea of History*. For interesting discussion see W. H. Dray. (1980), 'R. G. Collingwood and the Understanding of Actions in History', in

William Dray, *Perspectives on History*, London: Routledge &
Kegan Paul, 9–26; Patrick L. Gardner. (1952), 'The 'Objects'
of Historical Knowledge', *Philosophy*, 27, 211–20; Leon J.
Goldstein, 'Collingwood on the Constitution of the Historical
Past', in Krausz, 241–67, and also his (1970), 'Collingwood's
Theory of Historical Knowing', *History and Theory*, 9, 3–36,
and Nathan Rotenstreich. (1960), 'From Facts to Thoughts:
Collingwood's Views on the Nature of History', *Philosophy*, 35,
122–37.

History and human purpose

IH 309–15; PH 49–50; see Helgeby, ch. 7, van der Dussen, *passim*.

The inside/outside theory

IH 213–15; PH 217, see Dray, chs 2 and 3; Leach, ch. IX; W. H.
Dray. (1957–1958), 'Historical Understanding as Rethinking',
University of Toronto Quarterly, 27, 200–15; Patrick Gardner.
(1952), 'The Objects of Historical Knowledge', *Philosophy*, 27,
211–20.

Human history

IH 225–8, see Dray, ch. 4.

What and why

IH 210–17; see Dray, chs 2/4, Leach, ch. IX.

Re-enactment

IH Part V, Section 4, especially 215–19, 282–304, 441–50; PH
240, 244–5; see Dray, chs 2, 3 and 6, Leach ch. X, van der Dussen,
3.3.4, 3.3.5, 6.1 and *passim*, Helgeby, ch. 8; L. B. Cebik. (1970),
'Collingwood: Action, Re-enactment and Evidence', *Philosophical*

Forum, 2, 68–90; W. H. Dray. (1960), 'R. G. Collingwood on Reflective Thought', *Journal of Philosophy*, 57, 157–63; Leon J. Goldstein, 'Collingwood on the Constitution of the Historical Past', in Krausz, 241–67; Margit Hurup Nielson. (1981), 'Re-enactment and Reconstruction in Collingwood's Philosophy of History', *History and Theory*, 20, 1–31; Giuseppina D'Oro. (2004), 'Re-enactment and Radical Interpretation', *History and Theory*, 43, 198–208; Leon Pompa. (2002), 'Some Problems of Re-enactment', *Collingwood Studies*, IX, 31–44; W. J. van der Dussen. (1995), 'The Philosophical Context of Collingwood's Re-enactment Theory', *International Studies in Philosophy*, XXVII, 81–99.

Inference

IH 252ff., see Helgeby, ch. 8.

History and imagination

IH Part V, Section 2, esp. 241–9, 366–7; PH 151–4, 162–6; see Dray, ch. 6, Helgeby, ch. 9; W. H. Dray. (1983), 'R.G. Collingwood on the A Priori of History', *Clio*, 12, 169–81; David R. White. (1972), 'Imagination and Description: Collingwood and the Historical Consciousness', *Clio*, 14–28.

History and self-knowledge

IH 10–11, 18–19, 174–5, 226–7; PH 220–45; see Dray, chs 7 and 6, Helgeby, chs 6 and 7.

3 Arguing with Collingwood (1)

The problem of re-enactment

IH Part V, Section 4; see Leach, ch. X, van der Dussen, 8.2

The problem of the imagination in history

IH Part V, Section 2.

The problem of historical evidence

IH Part V, Section 3, esp. 385–90, 392–4, 456–9, 285–9; 'The Limits of Historical Knowledge' in Debbins, 90–103; PH 49–54, 231–2; see Dray, ch. 7, Helgeby, ch. 8, D'Oro, ch. 8, van der Dussen, 8.2 and *passim*; A. E. Burns. (1951), 'Ascertainment, Probability and Evidence in History', *Historical Studies: Australia and New Zealand*, 4, 327–39; L. B. Cebik. (1978), *Concepts, Events and History*, Washington, DC: University Press of America, ch. 3; Leon J. Goldstein. (1970), 'Collingwood's Theory of Historical Knowing', *History and Theory*, 9, 3–36; Joynt, C. B. and Rescher, N. (1959), 'Evidence in History and the Law', *Journal of Philosophy*, 56, 561–77; W. J. van der Dussen. (1991), 'The Historian and His Evidence', in van der Dussen and Rubinoff (eds), 154–69.

The problem of historical inference

IH 250–3, 262–3; PH 7–11, 79–82, 165–9, see Martin, ch. 10; Michael Krausz. (1980), 'Historical Explanation, Re-enactment and Practical Inference', *Metaphilosophy*, 11, 143–54; Donald S. Taylor. (1976), 'Literary Criticism and Historical Inference', *Clio*, 5, 345–70.

The logic of question and answer

IH 269–74, 485–7; PH 11–12, 240–1; AA 29–42, see Helgeby, ch. 4, Russell, ch. 1/A and *passim*; J. Somerville. (1989), 'Collingwood's Logic of Question and Answer', *The Monist*, 72, 526–41; R. A. Young. (1997), 'Collingwood's Logic of Questions and Answers', *Bradley Studies*, 3, 151–75; Peter Johnson. (2009), 'R. G. Collingwood and the Albert Memorial'. *Collingwood and British Idealism Studies*, 15, 7–40.

4 Arguing with Collingwood (II)

Past, present and future

IH 404ff.; PH 111–13, 189–91; for discussion see van der Dussen, 8.1 and *passim*.

The limits of history, thoughts and feelings

IH 204, 291–7, 306, 445–6; PH 67–9, and, more generally, Collingwood's discussion of the differences between thought and feeling in *The Principles of Art* (PA 157–60), where he issues a warning against over-simplifying the ways they are related. Collingwood writes,

> Thinking and feeling are different not only in that what we feel is something different in kind from what we think, nor also because the act of thinking is a different kind of act from the act of feeling, but the relation between the act of thinking and what we think is different in kind from the relation between the act of feeling and what we feel.
>
> (PA 160)

It is worth reflecting on the relevance of this warning to the possibility of re-enacting past feelings. For good and often thought-provoking discussion, see PH, Editor's Introduction, xxxiv–xli; Dray, 123–32; Helgeby, 152–7; Hughes-Warrington, 78–80; Johnson, ch. 3; Mink (1969), 92–106, 164 and *passim*; Mink, (1987), 234; Saari, 42–44 and *passim*; van der Dussen, 262–6. For further discussion, see W. H. Dray. (1997), 'Broadening the Subject-matter in The Principles of History', *Collingwood Studies*, IV, 2–33; L. O. Mink, 'Collingwood's Historicism: A Dialectic of Process', in Krausz, 154–78; C. B. McCullagh. (1990), 'The Rationality of Emotions and Emotional Behaviour', *Australian Journal of Philosophy*, 68, 44–58; L. Rubinoff. (1970), 'History and Perception: Reflections on R. G. Collingwood's Theory of History', *Philosophical Forum*, 2, 91–102.

Past lives

IH 295–6, 304–5; PH 69–75; PA 87; for commentary see Dray, 170, Hughes-Warrington, 80–1, Fred Inglis. (2009), *History Man, The Life of R. G. Collingwood*, Princeton, NJ: Princeton University Press, 23–33, 310–13; more generally, Roy Pascal. (1960), *Design and Truth in Autobiography*, London: Routledge & Kegan Paul; also useful are Peter Johnson. (1995), 'Intention and Meaning in Collingwood's Autobiography', *Collingwood Studies*, II, 12–42, and Lionel Rubinoff. (2006), 'R. G. Collingwood: Philosophy as Autobiography', in Thomas Mathieu and D. G. Wright (eds). *Autobiography as Philosophy, the Philosophical Uses of Self-Presentation*, London: Routledge, 230–52.

Facts and fictions

IH 240–6, 477–8; PH 152–3, 159–64, 184, 250n; PE 21–33, 35–48 (Collingwood's essays on Jane Austen), 107, 298–9; for discussion see Dray 201–7 for rules of method, 311–15 for narrative; Gallie 56–64 for narrative and rules of method especially useful for rule two; Mink (1987), esp. ch. 2; for a discussion which usefully sets Collingwood's views in the more general context of literature and culture see Phillip Smallwood, Editor's Introduction, PE xxiii–Iv, and also his (2000), 'Historical Re-enactment, Literary Transmission and the Value of R. G. Collingwood', *Translation and Literature*, 9/1, 3–24 and (2001), '"The True Creative Mind": R. G. Collingwood's Critical Humanism', *British Journal of Aesthetics*, 41/3, 293–311. For discussion of learning from literature see, for example, Peter Johnson. (2004), *Moral Philosophers and the Novel, A Study of Winch, Nussbaum and Rorty*, London: Palgrave Macmillan, esp. ch. 4.

History, politics and progress

IH, Part V, Section 6, 'History and Freedom'; Part V, Section 7, 'Progress as Created by Historical Thinking'; 'The Philosophy of Progress', *The Realist*, I, 1929, 64–77 (reprinted in Debbins, 1965, 105–20); A, chs VIII, IX and X, where we find, for example, 'The historian's business is to reveal the less obvious features hidden from a careless eye in the present situation. What history can bring to moral and political life is a trained eye for the situation in which one has to act' (A, 100). A good indication of Collingwood's views of inter-generational relations and progress is to be found in (1992), *The New Leviathan* (Revised Edition), edited with an introduction and additional material by David Boucher, Oxford: Clarendon Press, 497–8. For discussion of Collingwood on progress see Connelly (2003), 233–5; Helgeby (2004), 144–7; Browning (2004), 151–2; Hinz (1994), 202–6; Richard Murphy. (2008), *Collingwood and the Crisis of Western Civilisation, Art, Metaphysics and Dialectic*, Exeter: Imprint Academic, ch. 7, esp. 154ff. Jan van der Dussen. (1995), 'Collingwood on the Ideas of Process, Progress and Civilization', in Boucher *et al.*, 246–68. On the problem of justice in Collingwood's political philosophy see Peter Johnson. (2010), 'R. G. Collingwood and the Claims of Justice', *Collingwood and British Idealism Studies*, 1, 69–112, and also his (2010), 'R. G. Collingwood on Civility and Economic Licentiousness', *International Journal of Social Economics*, 37, 11, 839–57. For a modern liberal theory of inter-generational justice, see John Rawls. (1971), *A Theory of Justice*, (Revised Edition), Cambridge, MA: Harvard University Press, 1999, ch. V, 44, and for a criticism relevant to the argument here see B. M. Barry, 'Justice between Generations', in P. M. S. Hacker and J. Raz, (eds). (1977), *Law, Morality, and Society, Essays in Honour of H.L.A. Hart*, Oxford: Clarendon Press, 268–84; on non-human animals and history see M. Hughes-Warrington (2003), 82ff.

5 Receptions and reactions

For a general discussion on the reception and impact of Collingwood's ideas see David Boucher. (1995), 'The Life, Times and Legacy of R. G, Collingwood', in Boucher *et al.*, 1–31, esp. 16–18; Bernard Williams. (2006), 'An Essay on Collingwood', in his *The Sense of the Past, Essays in the History of Philosophy*, edited with an Introduction by Miles Burnyeat, Princeton, NJ: Princeton University Press, 352–72 is useful, and Inglis (2009), esp. ch. 10 where further responses may be found. For the reception of

The Idea of History see Jan van der Dussen, Editor's Introduction, IH, xxiii–xxviii; L. J. Cohen. (1952), 'A Survey of Work in the Philosophy of History 1946–1950', *Philosophical Quarterly*, 2, 172–86. Van der Dussen, (1981), 463–4, helpfully locates the early reviews of *The Idea of History*.

Collingwood's insights into the nature of history have found attentive listeners (both friendly and otherwise) in later twentieth-century philosophy of history, the methodology of the history of political thought, modern continental hermeneutics, especially the work of Hans-Georg Gadamer, the study of scientific revolutions and many other fields. Not all of Collingwood's influence in the area of historical studies derives from *The Idea of History*; thus, for example, the debate regarding the character of scientific revolutions owes more to the discussion of absolute and relative presuppositions in Collingwood's *An Essay on Metaphysics* (1940) than to *The Idea of History* itself. For a good discussion of this see Adrian Oldfield, 'Metaphysics and History in Collingwood's Thought', in Boucher *et al.*, 182–202. For discussion of Collingwood's influence on the developments in the methodology of the history of political thought, see James Tully. (1988), *Meaning and Context: Quentin Skinner and his Critics*, Cambridge: Polity Press, and more specifically, David Boucher. (1985), *Texts in Context*, Dordrecht: Martinus Nijhoff, esp. ch. 5.

For examples of the positivist view of history, see Patrick Gardner. (1959), *Theories of History*, New York: The Free Press, and many later editions, esp. Part II, 344–443. Discussion of the Hempel-Popper view of history, as it later came to be called, is to be found in William Dray. (1957), *Laws and Explanation in History*, Oxford: Oxford University Press; Dray (1995), ch. 3, *Re-Enactment and Laws*, is essential reading.

The papers on history delivered at the 1947 symposium may be found in 'The Character of A Historical Explanation', with contributions by A. M. MacIver, W. H. Walsh and M. Ginsberg, in *Proceedings of the Aristotelian Society*, Supplementary Volume XXI, 1947, 33–77. For Slotkin's review, see his (1948) 'Reflections on Collingwood's Idea of History', *Antiquity*, 22, 88, 98–102. For Murphy's review see Arthur E. Murphy. (1947), 'Review of R. G. Collingwood, The Idea of History', *The Philosophical Review*, LVI, September 1947, 587–92 (reprinted in *Reason and the Common Good, Selected Essays of Arthur E. Murphy*).

For Leo Strauss's review see his (1952) 'On Collingwood's Philosophy of History', *Review of Metaphysics*, 5, 4, June, 559–86; for an extended discussion of many of the issues mentioned here see Dray (1995), ch. 8. For an examination of Collingwood's indebtedness to Hegel see Browning (2004), esp. chs 4 and 6; for a comparison of Collingwood and Nietzsche see Hinz (1994), Part II. For discussion of Nietzsche in the context of Collingwood's social and political thought more generally see Richard Murphy. (2008), *Collingwood and the Crisis of Western Civilization, Art, Metaphysics and Dialectic*, Exeter: Imprint Acadamic, ch. 7.

For Michael Oakeshott's review see *The English Historical Review*, LXII, 1947, 84–6. Oakeshott's own account of history is best approached through his *Experience and Its Modes*, Cambridge: Cambridge University Press, 1933 and *On History and Other Essays*, Oxford: Blackwell, 1983. For Collingwood's discussion see IH 151–59. One should, perhaps, be a little wary of linking Collingwood's own thoughts on history too closely with those of his contemporaries, such as Herbert Butterfield who also wrote extensively on history, science, religion and politics. Butterfield certainly shared Collingwood's distaste for the picture of the historian as a spectator of the past, but he was nevertheless reluctant to accept his doctrine of meaning in history since he believed that in history, as Michael Bentley perceptively comments, 'there were "facts": he never doubted that one discovered them and he would not have understood Collingwood's proposal that they become generated by the questions one raises in making the inquiry.' Michael Bentley. (2011), *The Life and Thought of Herbert Butterfield, History, Science and God*, Cambridge: Cambridge University Press, 236.

Van der Dussen points out that the aim of a rapprochement between philosophy and history 'is well illustrated by Collingwood's historical treatment of the (criteriological) idea of history in *The Idea of History*.' (van der Dussen, 1981, 258). This is clearly the case, but it is worth also pointing out that the extent to which Collingwood's conception of philosophy lends itself to such a rapprochement also marks the distance between it and analytical philosophy. For an introductory treatment of Collingwood's conception of philosophy see Johnson, 1998, ch. 2. For the relation between Collingwood and analytical philosophy, see Michael Beaney. (2001), 'Collingwood's Critique of Analytical Philosophy', *Collingwood and British Idealism Studies*, 8, 99–122;

and for excellent recent discussions of Collingwood's conception
of philosophical method see Leach, 2009, Part 1; James Connelly
and Giuseppina D'Oro, Editor's Introduction, R. G. Collingwood.
(2005), *An Essay on Philosophical Method* (Revised Edition),
Oxford: Clarendon Press, a work that also contains a valuable
bibliography.

On Collingwood's philosophy of history and moral philosophy
see James Connelly. (2009), 'Collingwood's Moral Philosophy:
Character, Duty and Historical Consciousness', in William Sweet,
(ed.), *The Moral, Social and Political Philosophy of the British
Idealists*, Exeter: Imprint Academic, 233–49. For Collingwood's
influence on Alasdair MacIntyre, see MacIntyre's (1967) *A Short
History of Ethics*, London: Routledge & Kegan Paul, London
and later editions, and also his (1981), *After Virtue*, London:
Duckworth, and later editions. There are good discussions of
Collingwoodian themes in MacIntyre in the papers by Robert Stern
and Gordon Graham both in (1994), *After MacIntyre, Critical
Perspectives on the Work of Alasdair MacIntyre*, edited by John
Horton and Susan Mendus, Cambridge: Polity Press, chs 8 and 9.

For the relation between Collingwood's philosophy of history
and his archaeology, van der Dussen, 1981, Part 5 is essential
reading. Similarly important is P. W. M. Freeman. (2007), *The
Best Training Ground for Archaeologists, Francis Haverfield and
the Invention of Romano-British Archaeology*, Oxford: Oxbow
Books. Also valuable are Charles G. Salas. (1987), 'Collingwood's
Historical Principles at Work', *History and Theory*, 26, 1, 53–71;
Stein Helgeby and Grace Simpson. (1995), 'King Arthur's Round
Table and Collingwood's Archaeology', *Collingwood Studies*, II,
1–11; Grace Simpson. (1998), 'Collingwood's Later Archaeology
Misinterpreted by Beru and Richmond', *Collingwood Studies*,
V, 109–21, A. F. Wilson. (2001), 'Collingwood's Forgotten
Historiographical Revolution', *Collingwood Studies*, VIII, 6–72,
and Ian Hodder. (1995), 'Of Mice and Men: Collingwood and
the Development of Archaeological Thought', in Boucher *et al.*,
364–83.

For the philosophy of history after Collingwood see Keith
Jenkins. (1991), *Re-Thinking History*, London: Routledge, and
also his (1995), *On 'What is History?', From Carr and Elton to
Rorty and White'*, London: Routledge, which also contains a useful
list of further reading; Beverley Southgate. (1996), *History: What*

and Why, Ancient, Modern and Postmodern Perspectives, London: Routledge, and Gordon Graham. (1997), *The Shape of the Past*, Oxford: Oxford University Press. Even though Collingwood is not mentioned explicitly his influence is readily apparent. One modern book which does bring Collingwood alive in historiographical terms at least is John Burrow. (2007), *A History of Histories, Epics, Chronicles, Romances and Inquiries from Herodotus and Thucydides to the Twentieth Century*, London: Allen Lane, esp. Part V, ch. 26, 'The Twentieth Century'.

INDEX